Bill Miner...
STAGECOACH
& TRAIN ROBBER

by FRANK W. ANDERSON

Some of the weapons taken from Miner, Dunn and Colquhoun after the Ducks robbery. The Colt at upper left was one of the guns Miner carried.

PHOTO CREDITS
California Historical Society Library, 15, 19; Georgia Department of Archives and History, 49; Oregon Historical Society, 26-27; B.C. Provincial Archives, Inside and Outside Back cover, 3, 10, 12, 39, 42-43, 53, 58-59; Public Archives Canada, 4-5; Royal Canadian Mounted Police, 1, 3, 54-55; Vancouver City Archives, 8; Vancouver Public Library, 45; Wells Fargo, Inside Front cover; Donovan Clemson, 62; D. Shores, Front cover; Tourism B.C., Back cover.

PUBLISHER'S NOTE: In the original 1968 edition the author gave credit to the following people — some of whom are now deceased — and organizations for helping unearth the Miner story: T.W. Hall, Warden, British Columbia Penitentiary; Elizabeth Anne Johnston, head of the Library Association of Portland; James C. Bonner, Professor of History, Woman's College, Milledgeville, Ga.; Alice Wallace, Historian, State Historical Society of Colorado; B.F. Seymour, Records Officer, Department of Corrections, California; Major J.S. Mathews, Vancouver City Archives; and the Glenbow Foundation, Calgary, Alberta.

Additional thanks for the 1982 revision are due: Georgia Department of Archives and History; California Historical Society; California State Archives; Oregon Historical Society; B.C. Provincial Archives; RCMP Museum, Regina; and Cecil Clark, retired Deputy Commissioner, B.C. Provincial Police.

CANADIAN CATALOGUING IN PUBLICATION DATA

Anderson, Frank W., 1919-
  Bill Miner —, stagecoach & train robber

First published as: Bill Miner, train robber.
Calgary : Frontiers Unlimited, 1963.

ISBN 0-919214-18-5

1. Miner, Bill, 1847?-1913. 2. Brigands and robbers — Canada — Biography.
3. Brigands and robbers — United States — Biography. I. Title. II. Series.
HV6665.C3A52 1982   364.1'552'0924   C84-12710-3

HERITAGE HOUSE
PUBLISHING COMPANY LTD.
Box 1228, Station A
Surrey, B.C. V3S 2B3

Printed in Canada

PRINTING HISTORY
First printing 1963. Reprinted five times.
Revised edition 1982
Enlarged edition 1985
Reprinted 1989, 1992

CONTENTS

The police posse with Bill Miner, wrapped in blanket, and his two companions arriving at Kamloops courthouse on May 15, 1906, one week after their train holdup which netted $15. They were captured after a shoot-out in the Nicola Valley — shown on the outside back cover — after being found by Constable William Fernie.

Canada's
First
Train Holdup

A CPR train at Mission Junction during the era of Miner's holdup. The express and baggage cars are behind the coal tender.

Engineer N.J. Scott eased the throttle forward on Canadian Pacific Railway's big Transcontinental Express No. 1 and drew slowly away from the water tower 200 yards west of the depot at Mission Junction, British Columbia. The headlight's powerful beam made scarcely a dint in the pitch black night, with a dense fog restricting visibility even more. Already two and a half hours late because of the fog, the veteran trainman knew he would be even farther behind schedule before reaching Vancouver 65 km (40 miles) away. His watch showed 9:30 p.m. It was Saturday, September 10, 1904.

Intent on watching the twin ribbons of steel before him, Scott did not know that three men had boarded the crack express at the water tower and hidden in the blind baggage. His first awareness came when a hand was laid on his shoulder and a soft voice whispered, "Hands up."

Scott turned to see three men standing on the swaying platform in front of the coal tender. They wore soft brimmed hats and dark cloth masks with eye slits. Two carried a revolver in each hand and the third a rifle. Their leader appeared to be about five feet, nine inches tall and around 130

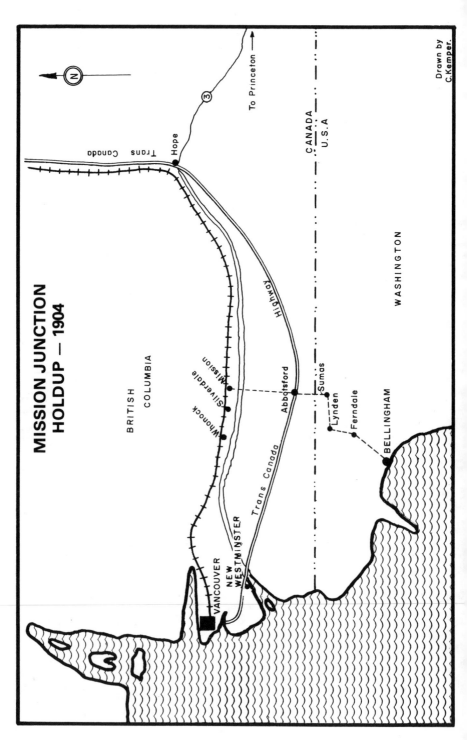

MISSION JUNCTION
HOLDUP — 1904

Drawn by
C.Kemper.

pounds. He spoke with a slow, southern drawl. The second man was slender, round-shouldered and dark haired. The third man, who carried the menacing rifle, was of medium height and build and square-shouldered. Their coolness marked them as experts at train holdups.

"I want you to stop the train at the Silverdale crossing," the leader said in his soft drawl. "Do what you are told and not a hair of your head will be harmed."

Realizing that the trio were serious, Scott nodded in agreement. "I am at your service," he replied, turning to the task of bringing the big locomotive to a smooth stop.

None of the men spoke until the train stopped at Silverdale siding. Then the leader motioned Fireman Harry Freeman down from the cab and escorted him back along the train to the express car behind the coal tender.

As they reached the express car, Express Messenger Herbert Mitchell opened the top half of his door and looked out. Seeing the fireman, he thought it was only a routine stop and withdrew, closing the door. The darkness and fog had prevented him from seeing the revolvers held by two men who followed Freeman.

"I knew when the engineer stopped the train just outside Mission that something was wrong," brakeman W.A. "Bill" Abbott later recalled. ". . . as I poked my head out of the car I came face to face with a masked fellow holding a gun that looked as big as a sewer pipe.

"He told me to get back inside unless I wanted my head blown off, and be quick."

Abbott did as ordered but managed to sneak away, plant signals to warn any approaching train then walk and run five miles to Mission to report the holdup. At Mission the agent refused to believe his story, convinced he was crazy or drunk.

On the train, meanwhile, news of the holdup caused wild confusion among the passengers. One report noted that the conductor collapsed from fright and one foolhardy man, despite the fog and darkness, fired a random shot towards the three men in the express car, but hit no one. Some passengers in the sleeping cars tore off their valuables, throwing them into spittoons or hiding them in crevices. Women screamed as the porter raced through shouting that the engineer had already been killed.

Unperturbed by the panic, the bandits ordered Freeman to uncouple the express car from the rest of the train. This done, they returned him to the engine where Scott was still under guard. "Go to the Whonock mile post and stop in front of the church," the leader instructed. "Do as you are told and no one will get hurt."

Scott slowly pulled the express car down the line and halted opposite the church at Whonock. Once again the engineer and fireman were left guarded by the man with the rifle while his two partners hurried back to the express car. Again Herbert Mitchell looked out but this time was able to see what was happening. He quickly closed the door and unearthed his revolver, a .38 Smith & Wesson.

"Open up or we'll blow the door down with dynamite," the older bandit shouted.

After some anxious moments the express car door opened. Mitchell

7

A B.C. Express stagecoach at Ashcroft in 1905. The stages served the Cariboo for half a century, carrying millions of dollars worth of gold with remarkably few holdups. Among this treasure was $62,000 in bullion from Consolidated Caribou Mine that Miner thought was transferred to the train he held up.

and a fellow employee jumped from the car, were searched and lined up beside the other members of the train crew. The leader appropriated Mitchell's revolver for his own arsenal.

"If you do what you are told, I won't harm a hair of your head," the leader drawled as he ordered Mitchell into the express car. "Now, open up that safe."

Mitchell did as he was told, although he was later unjustly fired because of the robbery.

The safe yielded a package containing $4,000 in gold dust consigned to the U.S. Assay Office in Seattle, a second package of gold dust worth $2,000 for the Bank of British North America in Vancouver, and about $1,000 in currency. Mitchell's travel grips were emptied and the loot placed in them. The leader roved through the express car, collecting registered letters and throwing them into the grips. He also tossed in an innocent looking parcel which contained $50,000 in U.S. bonds.

The main treasure the robbers were looking for, however, was thought to be $62,000 in gold shipped from the Consolidated Caribou Mine by stagecoach down the Cariboo Road to the Bank of British North America at Ashcroft on the CPR's main line. From Ashcroft the gold was to be transferred to the westbound train for the final 320 km (200 miles) to Vancouver. At the last moment, however, there had been a delay in shipment and the bullion was put on a subsequent train.

Thirty minutes after stopping the train, the bandits had finished looting the express car and sent their victims back to their posts. In order to slow the train and delay information of the robbery getting to Vancouver, the leader threw out the fireman's coal shovel. As he climbed from the train he cautioned Scott to reverse carefully and not run into anything since he had no rear lights.

As the big engine began to back up to rejoin the passenger coaches, the leader bade Scott and Freeman, "Goodnight boys," and disappeared into the darkness with his two partners.

When the train arrived in Vancouver, Engineer Scott and his crew were taken to the office of H.E. Beasley, Superintendent of CPR's Western Division. Here they were questioned by Chief Constable Colin Campbell of the B.C. Provincial Police and Inspector Chamberlin of the CPR Police. Since the crew described all three bandits as having American accents, it was obvious they were from the United States and, from their efficient method of operating, that they were experts. Descriptions of the three were broadcast by telegraph and later by newspaper, and a special train sent to the scene of the holdup.

Aware that this was the first train robbery in Canada, Chief Constable Campbell contacted the famous Pinkerton Detective Agency in the U.S. Although the B.C. Police force had been formed nearly fifty years before and had done an excellent job of keeping law and order, train robberies were new to them. By contrast, for nearly thirty-five years Pinkerton's had been running down stagecoach and train robbers all over the United States.

Superintendent James E. Dye, head of the Agency in Seattle, offered immediate help. He was still investigating a holdup of the Oregon Railroad and Navigation Company's express outside Portland, Oregon, on

September 23 of the previous year. He was intensely interested in the Canadian robbery, expressing the possibility that they had been committed by the same gang. Since Dye believed the holdup men would head south for the American border only 16 km (10 miles) from the crime, he dispatched agents into the area.

To encourage public cooperation in the hunt for the robbers, the CPR posted a reward of $5,000, as did the Federal government. The B.C. government added individual rewards of $500 apiece, bringing to $11,500 the reward for bringing Canada's first train robbers to justice. For many job holders of the era this sum represented up to twenty years' wages.

The B.C. Provincial Police on September 11 arrested a youth in the New Westminster freight yards because he was acting suspiciously. However, he proved to be innocent and was released. A more promising lead came from B. Shortreed, head of an Abbotsford posse, who found an abandoned boat adrift below Whonock where the holdup had taken place. They surmised that the men had used it to cross the Fraser River in their flight to the U.S. border. The posse searched the main road until they found footprints of three men at a point near the river below Whonock. The prints headed south through Abbotsford towards Lynden, Washington. Shortreed and his men followed them but near Sumas, just across the border, the prints veered into the bush and could not be traced.

Pinkerton's Superintendent Dye took over and scoured the region around Sumas, arresting a man named B.R. Davies on somewhat flimsy evidence. Davies, who had been in the district for three weeks, was observed

While lawmen including Pinkerton and CPR detectives and B.C. Provincial Police posses searched B.C.'s Lower Mainland for Miner, he had already returned to Princeton, above about 1900. Around the quiet Interior community he was George Edwards, a "southern gentleman in search of peace," even though there was a $11,500 reward for him.

to have been acting strangely. First he had rented a bicycle and toured the area between the CPR line and the border, asking pointed questions about train times and police posts. Then he had rented a horse and buggy and roamed the Sumas area south of the holdup site. Dye suspected Davies of having "cased" the job, though not actually taking part in it. For this reason he was held in custody in Bellingham.

While Dye was conducting his search, a second bold attempt was made to hold up the CPR Transcontinental on September 12. At a point close to the first robbery, ties were placed across the main line to stop or derail the train. Fortunately, the engineer noticed the barricade in time and backed up before anyone appeared. This action evidently frightened off the would-be bandits for they did not show up. The train crew were able to remove the obstacle and proceed on their way. This amateurish method of stopping the train led the police to believe that others, stimulated by the stories of bullion carried in express cars, had tried to emulate the daring trio.

Another more promising lead developed from Shortreed's investigation of the footprints from the bank of the Fraser River. On September 15, Superintendent Dye reported to the Provincial Police that three men had been trapped in a cabin near Ferndale, Washington, just across the border. Chief Constable Campbell hastened with his men to join the chase. But at that point, all leads dissolved abruptly.

First, the unfortunate B.R. Davies detained in Bellingham proved to be a detective working on another case. Then the "purloined" boat at Whonock which had directed the search towards the American border was found to be nothing more than one which had drifted free of its moorings. Worse, the three men in the cabin turned out to be legitimate homesteaders who had been in Seattle on the night of the Mission Junction holdup.

With all their leads gone, weary and disheartened Provincial Police returned to their respective posts, some having been without adequate food or sleep for three days. It was not surprising, therefore, that when there were indications that the three bandits had fled towards Princeton in the southern interior of B.C., they were discounted by the B.C. policemen.

Superintendent Dye returned to the Agency's Seattle office and added another footnote to one of the most famous files in the Pinkerton identification system — that of William A. Miner. Dye was convinced from descriptions given by the trainmen and from one almost insignificant clue that the man behind the Mission Junction holdup was the one who had planned the unsuccessful holdup of the Oregon Railroad & Navigation Company's express near Portland the previous September. There was only one man in Pinkerton's comprehensive files who was so polite while robbing a victim — and that was Bill Miner. Dye could not forget that when leaving the train, the bandit had warned Engineer Scott to back up safely and bade him goodnight. In addition, Bill Miner was known as the man who originated the phrase "hands up" and had been using it for almost forty years. The leader of the train robbers had used those words in greeting his victims in the Canadian holdup.

"I was positive," said Superintendent Dye later, "that Bill Miner was the mastermind behind the Portland train robbery and the holdup at Mission Junction in British Columbia."

Who was Bill Miner?

The man who called himself William A. Miner, among other names, was born between 1842 and 1847 — depending on the source of information. He told officials at San Quentin Prison that he was born in 1847, to those at the British Columbia Penitentiary he gave the year as 1842; while his tombstone records 1843. His nationality is equally confusing. The Pinkerton Detective Agency listed him as Canadian, while Canadian police claimed he was American. Both countries, it seems, were anxious to disown him.

Most accounts agree, however, that he was born at Bowling Green, Kentucky, in 1847. His father — whose family name was Macdonald — was said to have been a modest, law-abiding and industrious farmer. Miner had several sisters, one of whom married and moved to British Columbia, while two others raised families in Washington. After his death it was discovered that he also had a brother in B.C. who lived under an assumed name near Princeton.

Bill was said to have attended school to the age of sixteen, getting a good grounding in the fundamentals of reading, writing and arithmetic. From two grandmothers — one Catholic, the other Protestant — he obtained a strong base in religion and a respect for human life, and he developed a dislike for bigotry in any form.

After leaving school, Miner headed West, probably avoiding service in the Civil War of 1861-65. In later years he spoke of working in Texas, New Mexico and Mexico, and was variously a cowhand, prospector, and Pony Express rider. One authority on Miner, Cecil Clark, who spent thirty-five years in the B.C. Provincial Police before retiring as Deputy Commissioner, wrote in the *Vancouver Province* that Miner's career in crime started when he was sixteen and he "was to become the greatest in the business. His first holdup netted him $75,000 and for years it was Miner versus the Wells Fargo Express."

Miner said later that he was an Express rider at the time and the accessibility of the gold carried by the stages, plus his intimate knowledge of shipment dates, was too much of a temptation. He avowed that he received very little of this $75,000 and that most of the proceeds went to his gang. It is notable that even then he was spoken of as "the leader."

While there is doubt about the year of Miner's birth, one date in his early life that is established is April 3, 1866. That day in the County of San Joaquin he was sent to San Quentin prison for his part in the $75,000 stage-

13

coach robbery. The commitment paper is preserved in the California State Archives and states:

"This day again came the District Atty. and the deft, (defendant) who stands convicted of the Crime of Robbery was led to the bar in custody of the Sheriff. Thereupon the Court informed the defendant of the nature of the indictment found against him, his plea hereto, and the verdict of the jury thereon; And no legal reason being shown why judgement should not be pronounced; It is the judgement of the law as pronounced by the Court that the defendant William Miner be conveyed by the Sheriff of this County or his deputy to the State Prison, and that he be confined there for the period of three years, from the date of his incarceration."

On April 5 the nineteen-year-old entered grim San Quentin Prison at San Francisco. His inmate number — the first of five he was to acquire — was 3248; his new home noted for terror and brutality.

Prior to 1849, prisons in California were local, temporary, and informal. There was no need among the scanty population for a complex system of law enforcement and punishment. With the Gold Rush of 1849, however, a swarm of undesirable characters moved into the region, overfilling local jails. In desperation the authorities resorted to ships to house the increasing prison population but even this measure proved inadequate. In April 1851, they adopted a system of leasing out convicts to local contractors.

Spurred by the prospect of cheap labor, General Mariana Vallejo and General James M. Estelle purchased an old barkentine and contracted for fifty prisoners. The decrepit old craft was anchored off Point Quentin to be used as a boarding home while more permanent quarters were being built on the Point. The first building was a solid stone fortress which became known as the "Spanish Cell Block."

Local sheriffs took advantage of a regulation which paid them $1 per mile for transporting prisoners to the new prison. They crammed the ship with a miscellany of prisoners — male and female, literate and illiterate, dangerous and harmless. Disease was rampant, violence routine, escape attempts frequent. Unable to keep order, guards became zookeepers, relieving the monotony by drinking, gambling or consorting with the women prisoners.

In 1854, a local grand jury goaded the State Legislature to investigate. Little comment was made on the inhuman conditions within the Old Spanish Cell Block, but extreme concern was expressed at the lack of security. Under pressure of a public grown tired of escaped convicts, the Legislature acted to enforce security and discipline. A 20-foot wall was built around the prison and the institution turned over to John F. McCauley to operate at a profit.

Despite brutal methods and intimidation, McCauley failed to make the venture pay. In 1860 the State bought him out and took control of San Quentin. Four years later the desperate prisoners revolted, seized Warden T.N. Machin and escaped from their living hell. A citizen's army was mobilized to meet the crisis and the convicts were cornered and returned to their cells at the prison.

In retaliation, Warden Machin instituted a reign of terror. He had the

14

full support of the people of California, who lived in fear of the criminals and who desired an eye for an eye, a life for a life. Into this regime was thrust nineteen-year-old Bill Miner as a consequence of his first confrontation with the law.

Miner was issued a suit of unclean, tattered clothing. As a deterrent to escape and identification if he did, half of his head was shorn. Like the majority of the prisoners he was placed at work in the jute mill, the only revenue producing industry in the prison system.

Because of the extreme overcrowding and inadequate staffing, wardens were forced to rely upon convict bosses, a system which brewed corruption and sadism. Attempting to appease a vengeful public, the prison guards lived in fear of failure and this fear was passed on to the favor-currying convict overseers. Success was measured by profit and security, and every end was used towards achieving these objectives.

Punishments were frequent. At the time of Miner's 1866 confinement an average of ten public whippings a day was administered by the con bosses. Men were whipped not only for escapes or attempted escapes, but even for thinking of escape. Then for infractions such as a poorly produced piece of cloth from the jute mill, for "dumb insolence," and for talking back to a guard, there were additional punishments. Prisoners were beaten insensible with rubber truncheons, forced to stand for hours in a small circle painted on the floor, or subjected to the "hooks" — a torture used frequently by the more sadistic guards. In this punishment a prisoner's

San Quentin Prison in 1874. That year when Miner was returned after one of his escapes he was publicly flogged in the prison yard and thrown into the dungeon.

15

hands were bound behind him, then he was "hooked up" by his hands so that he was forced to stand on the tips of his toes. He was left until he collapsed.

When these punishments failed to quell a resolute spirit, the guards resorted to the "water cure" — high pressure hoses played on the convict's mouth and nose, suffocating him.

For victims of the various forms of torture there were no hospital facilities. The only care a prisoner could expect for injuries or ailments was that provided by fellow inmates.

Although Miner was originally sentenced to three years at San Quentin, on June 9, 1866, he was transferred to the Placer County seat at Auburn, California. Here he was convicted of a second count of grand larceny. His sentence was increased to five years, to run concurrent with the one he was serving. When Miner returned to the Spanish Cell Block a month later, he was given another close haircut, prison clothing and a new number — 3313.

On July 12, 1879, having served four years, three months and seven days behind bars, he was released to walk off into the California summer fog. For almost a year, Miner disappeared but he was busy, the terrors of San Quentin obviously forgotten. He roamed Calaveras County, California, holding up stagecoaches with a gun and formal courtesy. But the young holdup artist was about to become the victim of changing times.

Appalled by the ease with which desperadoes learned of large shipments of gold dust by stage, mine managers sought a safer means of transportation. While fast horses and heavily armed guards were a deterrent, robberies still occurred. The ruggedness of the country, its isolation, and its vastness made pursuit difficult and all too frequently useless.

The coming of the railroad promised an answer. Able to outspeed the fastest horses and offering built-in forts in the express cars, trains had many advantages over stagecoaches. As a result, mine owners started shipping their bullion by rail and holdup men had to evolve a method of successfully robbing a train. Several attempts were made, including trying to shoot the engineer. Invariably, however, the trains disappeared into the distance, defiantly belching black smoke.

A desperado named John T. Chapman evolved the most successful method of robbing a train. He quickly noted that gold was carried in express car safes, and that the express and baggage cars were always placed next to the engine. Chapman's method was to board the train at some isolated place when it stopped or slowed down, wait until the train was under way, then climb over the wood-filled tender and force the engineer at gunpoint to stop the train. To prevent intervention by crew or passengers who were invariably armed, the baggage and express cars were unhooked and taken a mile or two down the line.

Since express cars were locked and the attendants well armed, the next phase of the operation involved the use of dynamite — or at least the threat of its use — to open the doors. Once the attendants had complied they were forced to unlock the safes or have them blasted by dynamite.

In November 1870, Chapman and six accomplices wrote history of a kind when they used this method for the first time to rob a train in the

American West. The daring and successful robbery caused an immediate reaction, with the culprits hunted relentlessly by Pinkerton detectives. All except Chapman were eventually arrested and sentenced to prison terms.

The Chapman method became standard procedure over the years. From 1870 to 1933 there were fifty-nine train holdups in the United States and four in Canada. While there were some minor variations in the procedure — a derailment or placing an obstacle across the tracks — Chapman's method was the most effective and the least dangerous.

Because of the threat to a major source of revenue, the railroads increased their staff of detectives, turned more and more to the Pinkerton Detective Agency, and offered large rewards to encourage local sheriffs and posses to apprehend those responsible. As a result, only eight train holdups in the States, and one in Canada, remained unsolved between 1870 and 1933.

There is no record of Bill Miner being involved in any of the early train robberies in Canada. But that did not mean that he was leading a law-abiding life. Quite the contrary. He was active in California's Mother Lode country and as a result in mid-June 1871 was sentenced to ten years for robbery. He was escorted back to San Quentin and number 4902 was added to his criminal record.

The law had not finished with young Miner, however. On February 9, 1872, he was returned to San Andreas and convicted of another holdup. He received an additional twelve years. The following month Miner was back in San Quentin with another new number — 5206.

The prospect of all these years of living hell was evidently too much for Miner. On May 7, 1874, the prison bell clanged an alarm to the countryside. Bill Miner had escaped.

Freedom for Number 5206 was short. Within hours he was captured and returned to San Quentin. As punishment, he was publicly beaten in the prison yard and thrown into the dungeon.

The dungeon was actually a black tunnel about 15 metres (50 feet) long with seven small cells, or holes, on each side. There were no windows and the only entrance was through a solid door of hand-forged iron. Each cell — mere niches cut into the stone with bare walls and floor — had a solid iron door. There were no beds, no lights, and no ventilation, while a wooden bucket served as a toilet. Sometimes three or four men were confined to one cell, even though the only place to sit was a trianguler block of concrete in one corner.

The prisoners slept on the damp floor — with a blanket if they were lucky enough to get one and strong enough to keep it — and they received bread and water at the whim of the guards. When there was trouble, or too much noise, the dungeon guards threw lime on the cell floor, wet it then waited for the fumes to subdue the men.

Bill Miner was eventually released from the dungeon, but a close watch was kept on him. For years he wore a device known as the "Oregon boot" — a weight locked to his right leg to prevent further escape. After serving nine years and twenty-one days of his double sentence, Miner was discharged on July 14, 1880. He was thirty-three but had already spent virtually all of his adult life behind bars.

Bill Miner Versus Wells Fargo

When Bill Miner was released from San Quentin on July 14, 1880, he promptly left California for New Mexico. Here he worked a fall roundup for some ready money, then made his way to Denver, Colorado. It is possible that he also fitted a few stagecoach holdups into his schedule, for when he arrived in Denver he was calling himself William A. Morgan, the first of many aliases he was to adopt.

The pattern of his life was formed by this time. Unlike many men, the brutality of San Quentin did not seem to have embittered him. If his sojourn in the dungeon, the beatings, and the indignity and physical discomfort of the Oregon boot had any real impact on him, it was to imbue him with a tremendous desire to live.

In Denver, a prosperous mining community, Miner began to develop a new life — that of a distinguished gentleman from the South. His agile mind easily fabricated the necessary details, while his intelligence and education impressed those who met him. He gravitated to the saloons where his skill with a fiddle, his youthful, courtly manners and easy-spending ways made him a great favorite with the ladies. It also brought him to the attention of Billy Leroy, one of the best highwaymen of the Rocky Mountains.

Leroy had first appeared upon the Western scene with a $15,000 holdup of a stage in the San Luis Valley. Tracked to Kansas City and arrested, he was put under the escort of a U.S. marshal and placed on a train for Denver. During a trip to the lavatory, Leroy picked his handcuffs with the mainspring of his watch and leaped from the moving train. He successfully escaped and returned quietly to Denver. Events were to prove that he would have been far better to remain in hiding.

Both Leroy and Miner were slender men, well-dressed, quiet and handsome. Miner was the more intelligent and under his guidance the pair turned their attention to the Del Norte stage which operated from Del Norte, Colorado, along the Rio Grande River to South Fork and from there northward through Wagon Wheel Gap to Creede. At Creede the trail crawled upward through the Rockies for 90 km (50 miles), climbing Spring Creek Pass and over Slum Gullion Pass to Lake City. It was a punishing trip for horses, drivers and travellers.

After a few days of observation, the two men left Del Norte on a cool December evening in 1880 and rode out along the trail to conduct one of the most efficient stagecoach holdups on record. From it they gained $3,600 in gold dust and coin. After apologizing to the driver and passengers for the

Wells Fargo stagecoaches at Colfax,
California, in 1868. Miner's
first stagecoach holdup netted
him and his gang $75,000.

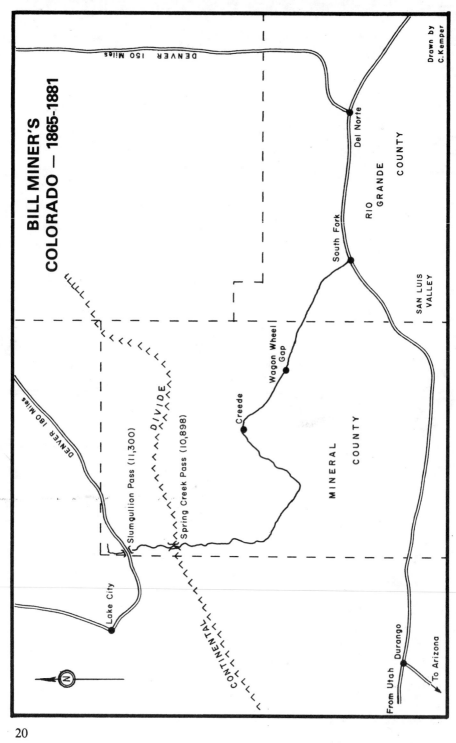

BILL MINER'S
COLORADO — 1865-1881

Drawn by
C. Kemper

DENVER 150 Miles

Del Norte

RIO
GRANDE
COUNTY

South Fork

SAN LUIS
VALLEY

Wagon Wheel
Gap

Creede

DENVER 180 Miles

Slumgullion Pass (11,300)

DIVIDE

Spring Creek Pass (10,898)

MINERAL
COUNTY

Lake City

CONTINENTAL

Durango

From Utah

To Arizona

N

20

ten-minute delay, Miner sent the stage on its way, admonishing the driver to be careful of the treacherous road.

A pursuit was immediately organized by hard-riding Lew Armstrong, sheriff of Rio Grande County. At one point the chase was so intense and the posse so close that Miner and Leroy were forced to separate. Both escaped, with the loot in Miner's possession. To recoup, Leroy attempted a second holdup of the Del Norte stage — this time with his younger brother. The pair were captured near Slum Gullion Pass and returned to Del Norte. Enraged by the two holdups, the citizens formed a lynch mob, seized the brothers from prison and hanged them. A photographer recorded the event.

After this near escape from the law, Miner left Colorado for the security of a larger center — Chicago. Here he bought two Saratoga trunks, filled them with male finery and departed.

He turned up in Onondaga, Michigan, in December 1880, some five months after his departure from San Quentin. But the only resemblance between the fashionably attired young gentleman of leisure with apparently unlimited resources and the former convict in tattered prison uniform were three tattoos. A charming depiction of a ballet dancer graced Miner's right forearm, two stars and a heart pierced by two daggers adorned his left arm, while a third mark was tattooed at the base of his left thumb. All had been noted by prison officials at San Quentin and later written into the files of Pinkerton Detective Agency. Meanwhile, the Agency was quietly linking a series of robberies committed in New Mexico and Colorado by a youthful bandit who always carried out his exploits with confidence and courtesy.

Unbothered by the accumulating mass of evidence, Miner proceeded to lionize the Onondaga community. The portals of society opened for the handsome young man with the square chin and keen blue eyes. He claimed to be a wealthy gentleman from California who was in the East winding up an estate to which he was the sole heir. His lavish spending lent credence to his story and at once established him as a great catch. He was quick to take advantage of the young ladies and became engaged to one dazzled-eyed damsel. His stories of houses in Sacramento and San Francisco, his tales of gold mines and ranches, and his undeniable charm left no doubt that he was everything he claimed to be.

But even in 1880, $3,600 did not last long with Miner's life style. By the end of February 1881, his funds were depleted. Inventing the fiction that his aged mother in San Francisco was ailing, he announced he was taking her on an ocean voyage ordered by the family doctor. At a banquet over which the mayor presided, his new-found friends gave him a royal send-off. Miner left for the West, promising to return to his tearful betrothed after his "urgent" business was completed.

In early March, Miner turned up in Denver, Colorado. He sold his finery, and replaced it with the more practical outfit of Levis, a Winchester rifle, two pistols and a hunting knife. He then contacted an old friend, Stanton T. Jones, who had a reputation for making life difficult and hazardous for stagecoach drivers.

Like most active robbers, Jones lived in near poverty between periods of prosperity. His enthusiastic greeting for his old friend cooled rapidly when he learned that Miner was as broke as himself. They nevertheless agreed to team up and, despite the lynching of Leroy and his brother, made plans to rob the Del Norte stage. By now they were so broke that their funds barely covered the stagecoach fare to Del Norte. Once there they left on foot to follow the Rio Grande River in the direction of South Fork.

Miner and Jones struck at dusk, holding up the stage a few miles out of town. Although they met no resistance from the driver or passengers, their loot was small. With his usual courtesy, Miner apologized for their intrusion, bade the driver goodnight and vanished into the dusk. Aware of Sheriff Armstrong's efficiency, they stole two horses from a nearby ranch and fled northward to the Continental Divide.

Unquestionably, many of the early bandits of the Old West, who confined their depredations to stagecoaches and trains, relied considerably on ranchers' and homesteaders' indifference to their trade. Many of the outlaws were generous to the isolated settlers and few, if any, preyed on them. But circumstances were changing. Prospects of large rewards and a growing awareness of law and order were altering the attitude of the settlers. As a consequence, when a bounty-conscious citizen of Creede noticed the two wanted men leisurely crossing a bridge near town, he sent a message to Sheriff Armstrong. Cautiously, Armstrong surrounded the pair and captured them without a struggle.

Armstrong tied his prisoners with wire, commandeered a passing freight wagon and started for the county jail at Del Norte, some 50 km (30 miles) away. Unable to complete the journey before nightfall, the party camped at Wagon Wheel Gap. The Sheriff left the prisoners in care of the relatively fresh wagon driver, unaware that Miner had a revolver which had been overlooked when he was searched.

An hour after midnight Miner pulled out his hidden six-shooter and forced the terrified teamster to untie them. As he and Jones slipped from the camp, the noise disturbed Armstrong. He reached for his rifle. Miner fired four shots. The first broke the Deputy Sheriff's arm, the second Armstrong's right arm at the shoulder, and the third and fourth struck the other deputy's arm. It was incredibly accurate shooting considering the darkness, and the first recorded instance of Miner using a weapon. As the Sheriff and his deputies crumpled under the gunfire, Miner and Jones faded into the darkness.

On stolen horses the pair fled south and west into Arizona. It was not long before stagecoach drivers were hearing for the first time the soft-spoken command "Hands up," and passengers receiving an apology in exchange for their wallets and pokes. Occasionally a victim caught sight of a dainty ballet dancer tattooed on the muscular forearm of the polite bandit. Gradually the Pinkerton files filled with additional information. An emerging pattern led them to believe that Bill Miner was the bandit and that he was working his way toward California.

The Pinkertons waited.

In the fall of 1881, Miner reached California. But since his arrival was not heralded by a rash of gentlemanly robberies, the Detective Agency suspected he was still in Arizona or neighboring Utah. In reality, Miner, or William Anderson as he now called himself, was holed up at Chinese Camp just inside the California border. Stricken with chills and high fever, he had

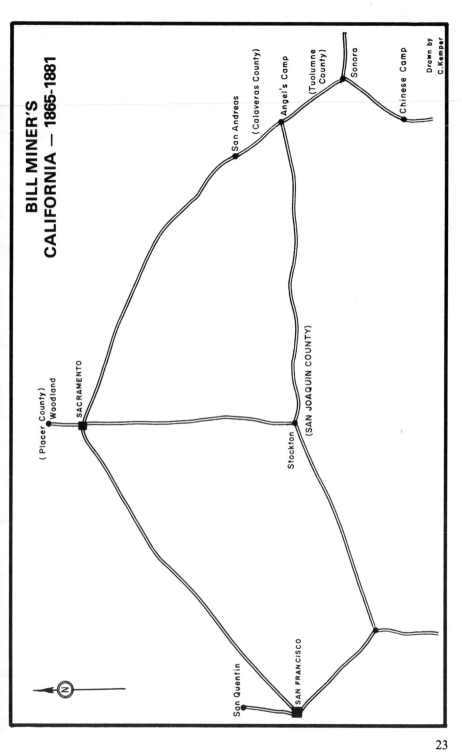

BILL MINER'S
CALIFORNIA — 1865-1881

N

(Placer County)
Woodland

SACRAMENTO

San Andreas
(Calaveras County)

Angel's Camp
(Tuolumne County)

Sonora

Chinese Camp

Drawn by
C. Kemper

(SAN JOAQUIN COUNTY)

Stockton

San Quentin

SAN FRANCISCO

been taken to the mining community by Jones. For days he hovered on the brink of death before his iron constitution and determination to live restored him to health. During his convalescence his kind, thoughtful manner and good spirits made him a host of friends.

Among the men who frequented Chinese Camp was a notorious horse thief named Jim Connor, well known to California sheriffs for his daring and resourcefulness. Another was Bill Miller, a slow-witted mountain of a man who owned a small ranch reputed to be a hangout for wanted men. Miller's constant companion was James Crum, also well-known, but relatively inoffensive.

After recovering from his bout with death Miner, still using his alias William Anderson, decided to replenish his empty pocketbook. The stage from Sonora to Milton which freqently carried hefty gold shipments from Angel's Camp mines looked promising. For this venture he needed help and because of his quiet manner and ability to plan a holdup he was soon leader of a gang that included Connor, Miller and Crum.

They settled on the stage as their first victim and the night before the holdup Miner and Connor boldly attended a country ball at Angel's Camp, already made famous by writer Bret Harte. In addition to checking the departure time of the stagecoach, Miner made a striking impression on one of the local belles who sang during the festivities. Miner told her he was leaving for San Francisco the following morning but promised to return. He also promised to send her some sheet music from the city — a promise that for Miner would have disastrous consequences.

The following morning, the Sonora-Milton stage was held up by four masked men not far from Angel's Camp. An iron box containing $3,250 in gold coins was lifted from the stage. One passenger had hidden a sack of gold dust worth $500 under a seat but it was not overlooked by the bandits. When the work was finished, Miner, with his usual expressions of regret at the delay, ordered the passengers into the stage and bade the driver move on.

The four men, anxious to put distance between themselves and the inevitable pursuit, headed west for San Francisco. At the halfway point, Bill Miller took a side road to his ranch while the rest rode hard to San Francisco.

In the meantime, Detective L. Aull, chief investigator for Wells Fargo, was dispatched to Angel's Camp with a Pinkerton man. It was soon evident that the robbery had Bill Miner's trademarks. The two lawmen quickly learned that Miner and Jim Connor had attended the dance. Connor was arrested but released after providing an alibi, while Miner's new girl friend promised to notify the detectives if he should contact her again.

For two weeks it appeared that Bill Miner and his three companions had made a successful escape. Then one morning the stage from San Francisco brought a package of music to the young woman at Angel's Camp. She notifed Detective Aull.

Aull returned to San Francisco and threw the full weight of Wells Fargo and Pinkertons into the hunt for the elusive Bill Miner. They discovered that Miner had purchased an expensive suit and overcoat, and a $190 gold watch and chain. The watch was exceptional because of its raised dial numbers. The investigators also learned that Miner had been seen only a day or two before their arrival and the name of his hotel. When they reached his hotel, however, they discovered that he had left the city to visit a woman. Suspecting that Miner was returning to Angel's Camp, Aull set out after him with two companions.

About the halfway point Miner, who was accompanied by James Crum, learned that the Wells Fargo detective was on their trail. Forsaking sonatas for safety, they turned aside and made their way to Bill Miller's Ranch. Unknown to them, Aull had received a message saying that Miller had been identified as one of the stagecoach robbers. Postponing his pursuit of Miner and Crum he, too, headed toward Miller's Ranch.

Early the next morning as he and his colleagues cautiously approached the ranch two men left the ranch buildings and ran towards a small ravine. The lawmen followed but as they were about to pass through a gate they were confronted by Jim Crum who covered them with a shotgun. But after several minutes of deadly debate, Crum realized that resistance was futile and surrendered to the law officers. When searched, he was found to have $600 in cash and two pistols.

After dispatching their prisoner to Sacramento, Aull and his aides resumed the search for the two fugitives, whom they expected to be Bill Miner and Bill Miller. Early in the afternoon, Aull, who was alone at the time, suddenly came upon the pair. Both bandits immediately covered him with their revolvers.

With great presence of mind, Aull — who was unknown to the fugitives — walked up to them carrying his shotgun loosely on his arm. He told them that he was out duck hunting and had mistaken them for members of his party. Miner laughed and said that they, seeing his shotgun, had taken him for a highwayman. After a few casual words, Aull returned to his buggy and drove off. But as soon as he was out of sight he circled back with William Arlington, approaching from a different direction. The Wells Fargo man fired a warning shot and called for their surrender. His demand was met by a volley of curses and blasts of gunfire. In the melee that followed, Miner slipped away and Miller surrendered. Aull left his prisoner with Arlington, pursued Miner and after a second gun battle persuaded the outlaw to surrender.

The three men were questioned separately in Sacramento. Miller and Miner remained silent during the interrogation, but Crum faltered. He confessed to the Sonora stagecoach holdup, implicating Stanton Jones as well as Miner and Miller.

On December 15, 1881, at Sonora, Miner was convicted of stagecoach robbery. Because of his long record of robbery and evidence of the Pinkertons, he received the maximum twenty-five years. Miller, who also possessed a long list of proven or suspected felonies, received a similar sentence. Crum, because of his confession and evidence, was sentenced to twelve years. Jones, the fourth member of the gang, left San Francisco before he could be apprehended and was never arrested for the crime.

On December 21, 1881, Bill Miner walked through the gates of San Quentin once more. He was No. 10191.

Fiasco on the Portland Express

The Oregon Railroad and Navigation Company's Chicago to Portland Express in 1900. After Miner's abortive attempt to rob the railway he escaped north to the Nicola Valley-Princeton region of British Columbia. Years after his death the reason surfaced — his brother lived near Princeton under the assumed name of Jack Budd.

There were few changes in the prison system when Bill Miner returned to begin his sentence of twenty-five years. Mindful of his previous escape, prison authorities branded him a troublemaker and watched him closely. As the years passed with Miner working in the prison jute mill and causing no problems, it appeared that he was resigned to completing his heavy sentence. One day, however, the prison bell tolled the alarm. Miner had made his second escape from San Quentin.

After only a few hours of freedom he was recaptured. This breakout cost Miner all his accumulated good time — at that point four years and three months — and he was thrown into the dungeon. Here he remained so long that, like the concrete block in the corner of the cell, he almost became a fixture.

Finally on June 17, 1902, having served nineteen years, five months and twenty-seven days of his sentence, Bill Miner walked out of San

Quentin for the third time. It was also the last time, though not because Miner had decided to become law-abiding.

The almost solitary confinement, the frequent beatings, the lung-corroding gases from the watered lime used to quell disturbances in the dungeon, and long deprivation of sunlight would have broken a lesser man, but not Bill Miner. Somehow he had retained his ability to smile, to dampen the rages of hate that swept through him at the indignities he had suffered.

Although now fifty-four, Miner was still formidable. His face was hardened by self-discipline, his blue eyes still surveyed the world unafraid, his agile mind still worked ceaselessly behind an innocent and beguiling smile. His prison years had sharpened his intuitive senses, giving him the ability to evalute other men quickly and to manipulate them.

Miner quickly dropped his own name for one of his aliases, Bill Morgan, and left California for his sister's home at Whatcom, just east of Bellingham in Washington. A few miles away at Samish Flats lived another sister. He obviously needed time to rest and to think.

The world Bill Miner knew prior to his long incarceration had changed considerably. The Wells Fargo stage lines were nearly history. Gold bullion moved by trains which were now bigger, faster and better guarded. The countryside was more populated and tracking fugitives was made easier by newspapers and a telegraph network. In addition, the increased use of photography by Pinkertons provided almost instant identification.

Most criminals of Miner's age would have retired, but Miner wasn't like most criminals. He formed an acquaintance with seventeen-year-old Charles Hoehn, an orphan who lived in a co-operative colony in Whatcom.

Towards the middle of September 1903, Miner took Hoehn to a circus in Portland, Oregon. From there they went to the community of Gobi where Miner acquired a second companion, a man who called himself Williams. The trio moved into a fisherman's shack on Government Island where Miner outlined his plans for a train robbery.

A few days later, Miner and Williams slipped from the shadows of the Portland freight sheds and boarded the Oregon Railroad and Navigation Company's crack express. They remained hidden until the train reached Troutdale, a small way station a few miles out of Portland. Then they moved, crawling over the tender to surprise Engineer Ollie Barrett and Fireman H.F. Stevenson. Covering the trainmen with revolvers, Miner ordered them to continue to Mile Post 21 and to stop the train at a light. It was 9.30 p.m.

Young Charles Hoehn, carrying two long poles to which sticks of dynamite had been tied, came out of the darkness. Ordering Engineer Barrett to carry the dynamite, Miner and Williams escorted the trainmen to the baggage car. Hoehn, meanwhile, took up a position on the opposite side of the train and fired a warning shot to keep inquisitive passengers inside.

When a request to open the baggage car went unheeded, Miner seized the poles, lit the fuses and placed the dynamite against the door.

Miner's mistake in dynamiting the baggage car instead of the express car containing the safes made it obvious that this was his first attempt at train robbery. In addition, he was nervous and swore violently at the least obstruction. Following the explosions which blew the door in, he and his companion made a second mistake. Instead of herding the trainmen as a shield, Williams rushed ahead while Miner followed with the engineer and fireman.

The express car messenger, now fully alerted, leaned from the car with a shotgun. As the quartet approached he blasted into the darkness, hitting Williams in the head and Engineer Barrett in the shoulder. Williams dropped while Barrett was slammed against the side of the car. A quick shot from Miner's revolver drove the messenger inside.

As Barrett cried out in agony for the messenger to stop shooting, Miner dropped to his knees beside his companion. A cursory examination indicated that Williams was dead. Ordering the engineer and fireman back to their cab, Miner collected Hoehn and disappeared down the embankment toward the Columbia River which paralleled the railway.

When the posse arrived at the scene the following morning, they found Williams still alive. He gave his name as Jim Connors, his age twenty-five, and Portland as his place of residence. Beyond that, he refused to speak.

Sheriff Storey of Portland officially took up the chase, but in spite of arresting several young men no real progress was made. Meanwhile, Captain Nevins of the local Pinkerton Detective Agency seemed to have information the Sheriff did not possess. He pursued a separate line of inquiry. About October 1, a detective turned up at a lumber mill in Whatcom, showing a decided interest in a young man who called himself Charles Morgan. Then on October 9, "Williams" finally talked. He told the Sheriff his real name was Guy Harshman and that there were four other men in the gang. He identified them as Jim James, a distant cousin of Jesse James; George Underwood; Bill Morgan and his nephew, Charles. Harshman said that James and Underwood had fled to Mexico, but that the Morgans could be located in Whatcom.

Sheriff Storey hastened north to Whatcom.

Coupled with Harshman's confession and the information the Pinkerton detective had discovered, Sheriff Storey arrested Charles Morgan and identified him as Charles Hoehn. At the home of Bill Miner's sister they found a blood-stained overcoat that had belonged to Harshman, and learned that the "Morgan" of Harshman's confession was really Bill Miner. Despite an intensive search, no trace of Miner was found.

On November 15, 1903, Charles Hoehn was sentenced to ten years for his part in the holdup. Guy Harshman, still partly paralyzed from being shot, was imprisoned for twelve years. But the mastermind of the robbery had vanished. All the frustrated Pinkerton Detective Agency could do was add another chapter to the voluminous file of William A. Miner.

In the meantime a slender man who spoke with a soft accent appeared at Princeton in the southern interior of British Columbia, some 280 km (174 miles) from Vancouver. He said his name was George W. Edwards and that he was a southern gentleman in search of peace and a compatible climate. He moved in with the Schisler family who had a farm on Bald Mountain not far from Princeton.

Years later one of the Schisler daughters, Millie, wrote of the incident. "A neighbor of ours by the name of Bob Tilton brought a man to our place by the name of George Edwards. He wanted to stay at our place for the winter. So my father said he could. We all liked him very much and he was a perfect gentleman and so good to us kids. He often gave us a quarter when we went to school in the morning. We thought that was a fortune.

"Well, in the spring he said he had to go to South America to his gold mine and even took out the map and showed us where it was. He left a lot of things with us and said to mother if I don't come back you can have them. He came back in a few weeks and said he was going to move up and stay with Jack Budd . . . ."

Jack Budd lived close to the Schislers. He was a bent, grey-haired little man, originally from Texas, where he claimed to have know the affable George Edwards. Budd arrived in B.C. for the gold rush to Granite Creek in the mid-1880s. After horse-trading at Aspen Grove and Douglas Lake in the Nicola Valley, he had taken up homesteading near Princeton in 1898.

Of him, Millie Schisler later wrote: "He was here when we came in 1900. Mr. George Aldous and him owned a hotel then and were partners. The hotel burned down and he took up a piece of land on the 5 mile range near the Bald Mountain. Then, when Coalmont started up Jack Budd and a fellow by the name of Ed Pringle started a livery stable. That didn't do so well so Jack Budd went back to his farm on the hill and lived there until he died . . . ."

(After Budd's death, Princeton residents were astonished to learn something else about him and why he admitted knowing George Edwards in Texas. The two, in reality, were brothers.)

After Bill Miner, or George Edwards, moved in with Budd his skill with a fiddle made him a welcome addition to the social life of the area and his charm attracted young and old alike. The very essence of a southern Colonel, with a flowing white mustache and mane, he proceeded to do a little cattle buying, a little prospecting, and a little farming, but mostly he made friends.

Among the noted characters then around Princeton was a short, stocky man — William "Shorty" Dunn, or Thomas William Dunn. He had been prospecting off and on in the Hedley area and at the time of Miner's arrival was working in a sawmill just outside Princeton.

Miner took a special interest in Dunn, presenting him with a watch and a gun, and taking him on several bear hunting expeditions or on cattle drives to the coast. When one of these trips coincided with a train holdup at Mission Junction in September 1904, no one dreamed of connecting the genial Mr. Edwards, nor his companion, Shorty Dunn, with the robbery.

After the Mission Junction holdup, Miner returned to Princeton with Billy Dunn and settled on Jack Budd's small ranch. As he had done previously in the United States, he entered fully into the role of a southern gentleman of means and leisure.

W.R. Nelews, station agent at Princeton, recalls: "Bill Miner . . . used to spend about three hours every day grooming and training his beautiful white horse named Pat. I believe no one could have a greater love for his mate than each had for the other. Pat had an intelligence of a very high order. Miner had a specially constructed watch, whose dial letters were raised, and had trained his horse to tell the time by stamping his feet . . . Bill was a great favorite with children. Saturday afternoons, weather permitting, Bill and Pat, followed by a bunch of girls and boys, would go to the outskirts of Princeton and the children would be given tickets for a free ride on Pat. Pat took as much pleasure from these rides as the children did."

One of these children grew up to become Mrs. Mazie Hurley who remembered Miner well: ". . . he was quiet, well educated, grizzled, with keen steel blue eyes, gentle and kindly mannered with women and children, a dead shot and a fine horseman . . . . In the winter of 1905 . . . there was not much to amuse myself with outside of hunting and riding. I had no companion of my own sex, except a couple of little Indian girls. So Bill spent two days clearing a place on the Dodds' field and flooding it from a little stream which flowed through to make a pond for me to skate on."

In November 1905, the same year that the "southern gentleman" built the skating rink for Mazie, the Great Northern train was held up at Raymond brickyard near Seattle, Washington. Three masked men got away with $30,000.

P.K. Ahearn, head of Pinkerton's Seattle bureau, was convinced it was a Bill Miner job. Later, residents of Princeton recalled that George Edwards was away on one of his frequent trips to the coast at this time with Shorty Dunn.

In the meantime, Miner continued his peaceful ways. He did not frequent the little town of Princeton to any extent but spent most of his time among the scattered population. Bags of candy for the children and elaborate boxes of chocolates and other gifts for the older members of the family endeared him to all. For a while he worked at the famous Douglas Lake Ranch, but at no time did he seem pressed for money.

Somewhere along the way, Bill Miner acquired a second companion. In the spring of 1906, Louis Colquhoun, a former schoolteacher, dropped in at the Budd ranch. Louis was a good-looking, easy-going young fellow with gentlemanly manners who had been born on a farm near Clifford, Ontario. As a young man he taught school for two years but contracted tuberculosis and came west to Calgary where he found employment in a warehouse and then with a survey crew. From Calgary his wanderings took him to Vancouver and then San Francisco. While in the States, he acquired a two-year sentence in Walla Walla Penitentiary for petty theft. Back in Canada, he worked at various jobs in the Interior of British Columbia. While employers liked him and gave him good character references, most of them felt he lacked ambition.

On Jack Budd's Ranch he found the type of work he liked best — doing nothing with genial companions.

One morning in March 1906, Miner and Shorty Dunn dropped into the McFadden Ranch at Princeton and told the rancher that they were going on a prospecting trip towards Kamloops and expected to be gone at least three weeks. McFadden, with typical frontier generosity, loaned them a dark bay and a pinto to use as pack horses.

A month later, on April 29, Miner, Dunn and Colqhhoun appeared near Ducks (now called Monte Creek), a small way station 25 km (16 miles) east of Kamloops. They bought supplies from a local store and stated that they were prospecting. What they didn't say was that the prospecting involved not minerals but a train.

Disaster at Ducks

A Canadian Pacific transcontinental express showing the coal tender where Miner and his companion hid and the express and baggage cars. At Ducks the robbers mistook the baggage car for the express car — with disastrous results.

Bill Miner

Shorty Dunn

Louis Colquhoun

The night of May 8, 1906, was dark, accentuated by smoke from a forest fire burning in the mountains north of Ducks. The Canadian Pacific Railway's Imperial Limited, westbound for Vancouver with Engineer J. Callin at the throttle, made its routine stop at the station, then pulled out. As the big locomotive was gathering speed, Callin noticed two men crouching on the coal tender. When he asked what they were doing, the men scrambled down from the tender and levelled revolvers at him and Fireman A. Radcliffe.

"Don't do anything foolish and you won't be harmed," one warned in a soft voice. "Stop the train at Mile Post 116."

He was masked with a dark handkerchief and wore goggles and a black slouch hat. The other man had a handkerchief over the lower part of his face and wore a sweater and dark trousers.

Callin stopped the train at Mile 116, west of Ducks. Here a third man came running across the field. He wore no mask but had the neck of his sweater pulled up and his cloth cap pulled down. Despite these precautions, his face was clearly visible in the light from the open firebox of the engine. Under his arm he carried a parcel of dynamite wrapped in newspaper. The time was 11:30 p.m.

There was no commotion from the passengers as Fireman Radcliffe was taken back to uncouple the first car. After his return to the cab, the leader stated "I want you to stop at the flume," indicating a spot about 300 yards ahead. Here the trainmen were ordered from the engine and they approached the adjacent car in a group.

Inside the mail car were clerks A.L. McQuarrie and W.M. Thorburn. No resistance was offered by either man and they left the car and permitted themselves to be searched. Thorburn, who had been involved in the 1904 Mission Junction robbery, instantly recognized the leader as the same man who had masterminded it, but managed to conceal his start of recognition.

While one man stood guard over the prisoners, the other two went inside with McQuarrie. "You're somewhat ahead of your time," one remarked to Callin. "We didn't expect you for another hour. Lucky we were waiting."

Callin explained that the change over to summer service had just begun and that the train was running in two sections. This was the first section.

In the flickering glow from three acetylene lamps in the mail car, the leader searched the compartments until he found the registered mail. There were only eleven letters in the sack.

"Where is the shipment for San Francisco?" he demanded. "The registered mail for Frisco?"

McQuarrie answered that there was no mail for the California city. One of the robbers who had been browsing through the car suddenly exclaimed: "This isn't the express car! It's the baggage car!"

The leader swore and made a violent movement with his revolver which dislodged his mask and gave McQuarrie a good look at his face. He quickly readjusted the mask, but the damage had been done.

"We must have left the express car back with the rest of the train," he grumbled. "Well, let's see what's here."

He passed up several small, flat packages on a shelf, believing from the way they were piled that they were valueless. Unknown to him, they contained $40,000 in bank notes. But a package of liver pills attracted his attention and he broke it open, passed several to one of his companions and pocketed some himself.

The job finished, he ordered the engineer to advance to a spot between Mile Posts 119 and 120. There he and his cohorts took their leave. As Callin prepared to return to the stalled coaches, the leader called cheerily: "Goodnight, boys. Take care of yourself."

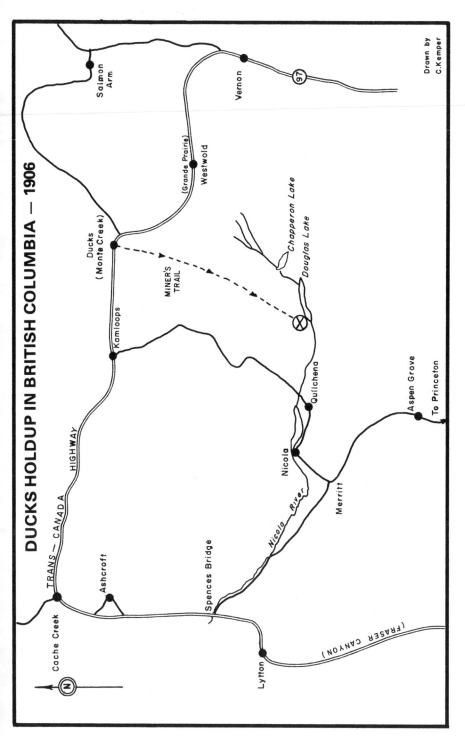

DUCKS HOLDUP IN BRITISH COLUMBIA — 1906

Drawn by
C.Kemper

Salmon Arm

Vernon

(97)

(Grande Prairie)

Westwold

Ducks
(Monte Creek)

Chapperon Lake

Douglas Lake

MINER'S
TRAIL

Kamloops

TRANS — CANADA   HIGHWAY

Quilchena

Ashcroft

Cache Creek

Spences Bridge

Nicola River

Nicola

Merritt

Aspen Grove

To Princeton

Lytton

(FRASER CANYON)

N

35

Little could be done that night by way of pursuit, but the following morning the Provincial Police were on the job. Constable W.L. Fernie, a man recognized as a top tracker, found a parcel of dynamite wrapped in a page of the Kamloops *Inland Sentinel* newspaper lying beside the track. The paper carried the mailing label of an Aspen Grove subscriber. He also noted that three sets of tracks — one smooth and womanish, the other two masculine and hobnailed — led from the railway between Mile Posts 119 and 120.

Enlisting the assistance of the Indian scouts, Fernie followed the tracks to a camp behind the Buse Ranch. The site was secluded but commanded a good view of the CPR tracks. There were no footprints leading away from the campsite, however, and the hard-baked ground afforded little sign of passage.

Because of forest fire raging in the mountains to the north behind Ducks, Fernie reasoned that the men would have to go south through Douglas Lake country. He and the scouts circled southward from the campsite and picked up the three sets of prints, now accompanied by the marks of two horses. They followed them without difficulty to Campbell's Meadows where they found a fresh campsite.

Positive that the train robbers were making for the United States border, Superintendent F.S. Hussey of the B.C. Police wired to Calgary for assistance from the Royal North West Mounted Police. In response, a party of eight Mounted Police under Assistant Commissioner A. Bowen-Perry arrived in Kamloops, bringing with them their saddles and bridles but wearing civilian clothes. Under Sergeant Wilson they set out in pouring rain, although not before the untrained range horses provided a bucking demonstration in the downtown area.

In addition to members of the two police forces, many other people were involved in the search.

"Men are out in every direction and all the roads and trails north and south, through the Nicola and Okanagan districts, are watched," noted the Kamloops *Inland Sentinel* in its front page story of the robbery. "A number of Pinkerton detectives came in from Seattle yesterday and have joined in the chase. F.S. Hussey, superintendent of Provincial police, arrived here last night to take charge of affairs and railway detectives and officials are also in the city, directing the search and placing all their resources at the command of the police."

The paper carried a description of the three, with that of Miner's flattering him. He was described as "A man about 5 feet, 6 inches tall, fairly well built, apparently young, dressed in an old sweater."

The *Inland Sentinel* also noted that the searchers had found three camps ". . . one the first day, an old camp which had evidently been headquarters while preparing for the robbery as there is a well beaten track from it to the railway. The one found yesterday morning, when they got the two horses, was higher up the hill and the posse passed within one hundred yards of it the night before. They must have disturbed the robbers who shifted their position to another camp found at 5 o'clock this morning and where they found a handkerchief, a piece of candle and a scrap of a letter and a piece of the Manitoba Free Press of April 10th.

"At the camp found yesterday they found, besides the two horses, a $30 saddle, flour and other provisions, clothing, etc. The horses were hobbled American fashion, one hind and one fore foot. The same horses were seen on Monday by cowboys several miles on the Nicola road, and the supposition is that the animals wandered farther from camp than the robbers anticipated and when they wanted them they could not find them, otherwise they would have been further away ere this . . . ."

The miscalculation which resulted in the loss of the horses was a grave setback for the robbers. They now had to escape on foot, in little more than the clothes they wore. They took their guns but left most of their food at the abandoned campsite.

Worse, the trail they left was distinctive since it consisted of the two sets of hobnail boots and a slim, smooth imprint — the one who made it obviously wore special shoes. But the country the train robbers were passing through was wooded and rocky so that the tracks were indistinct. To further confuse those tracking them they walked on their heels in areas where the ground was soft.

Constable Fernie and his scouts nevertheless continued their determined pursuit. They had now been following the trail for 72 hours in pouring rain — losing the three sets of prints, finding them again, cursing at the delay. They realized that once the fugitives left the woods above Douglas Lake Ranch and got onto the plains, tracking would be almost impossible.

By the forenoon of May 14, Fernie came to the edge of the timber. Unable to decide which of many routes might have been taken by the fleeing robbers, he ordered Constable Pearse, who had joined them at Campbell's Meadow, to go towards Grande Prairie (now Westwold) in the Okanagan while he continued toward Douglas Lake. He left the Indian scouts behind as there were now no tracks to follow. Fernie, however, had picked the correct route for his search.

As he later recalled: "I was moving rather slowly, while keeping a sharp lookout for the bandits, when suddenly I came upon them. They had not seen me so to be sure of their identity I went back upon their trail until I assured myself that the tracks were the same as we had been following from the scene of the holdup. There they were, the two with hob-nailed boots and the slim, womanish smooth shoes of the third. I knew then that we were sure of our men, so I rode back towards Chapperon Lake to secure mounted police assistance . . . ."

Unknown to him, Fernie had also been spotted but because he was dressed in civilian clothes his real identity was not realized by the bandits. One was positive that Fernie had seen them and wanted to kill him, but the others vetoed the idea.

Guided by Fernie, the Mounted Police posse under Sergeant Wilson arrived at the place where he had observed the fugitives, but it was bare. Realizing it would only be a matter of time before the police overtook the bandits, Fernie left them and returned to look after the Indian scouts.

The Wilson patrol spread out and worked its way towards Quilchena. Shortly after 1 o'clock, having covered scarcely a mile and a half, Corporal Stewart suddenly threw up his arm. Ahead three men were seated on the ground eating lunch. As the police closed in they showed no concern.

"Who are you?" Wilson demanded.

"I'm George Edwards," Bill Miner replied. "This is Billy Dunn and the tall one is Louis Colquhoun."

"What are you doing here?"

"Prospecting," replied one of them. "We started over at Aspen Grove and worked our way towards Grande Prairie and we haven't had any luck so we're on our way back to Princeton."

Wilson debated. The trio did not act like wanted men. Finally, he decided to move boldly and stated that they were under arrest for train robbery.

Bill Miner protested with a laugh, "We do not look much like train robbers."

But at that moment Miner's bluff ended. Shorty Dunn suddenly shouted "Look out boys, it's all up," and fired his .45 Colt. Before Miner or Colquhoun could react, they were covered by the posse.

Dunn scrambled to his feet, still firing wildly as he headed for the brush with three police in pursuit. Suddenly, he threw up his hands, "I'm shot!" The .45 fell from his hand as he toppled into a ditch, hit in the leg. He was quickly disarmed of a second revolver and taken from the ditch.

Convinced by Dunn's reaction that they had their men, the police made a careful search of the campsite. It produced more firearms, including a rifle, and on Miner a pair of goggles and several packets of pills. More significant, however, was that Sergeant Shoebotham recognized Miner from a description on a $20,000 reward poster. Corporal Browning also remembered the poster which he and Shoebotham had discussed two months earlier. As he was tying Miner's hands behind his back he recognized the tattoo at the base of his left thumb. The police were now certain that George Edwards was, in reality, one of North America's most wanted stagecoach and train bandits.

The police returned with their captives to the Douglas Lake Ranch and borrowed a buckboard from manager Greaves who assured them that a mistake had been made. He identified Miner as George Edwards, a well-known rancher and prospector. Dunn he knew only slightly, and Colquhoun not at all.

Unconvinced, Sergeant Wilson took his prisoners to Quilchena where Dunn's wound was attended by a doctor. After a night's rest the party left for Kamloops. They arrived on the evening of May 15, one week after the Ducks holdup. *The Kamloops Standard* later reported:

"On Wednesday afternoon at half past four a thousand people stood in the rain to watch a bedraggled cavalcade jogging down the hills back of the town. Two yellow clad policemen — they were wearing their oilskin raincoats — formed the vanguard of the procession. A wagon came next in which sat three men charged with train robbery, and the wagon was surrounded by more of the yellow clad horsemen.

The Kamloops courtroom during the trial. Miner, his chin on his hand, and Colquhoun are in the prisoner's box, with Dunn sitting outside. Beside Dunn is CPR detective R. Bullock, while at right center defence lawyer Alex D. McIntyre leans forward.

"Arriving at the jail, nine weary men slipped from the saddles and as many tired and dripping horses shook themselves till their trappings rattled like castenets. A few minutes later the watching crowd saw the prison doors close upon the men who it is now fully believed held up train 97 on May 8th.

"Constable Fernie, to whom the capture is due, was with the police and waited until he saw his men safe behind the bars. He has been night and day on the trail since the robbery. Once the prisoners were in the Warden's office the process of entering them upon the jail records was proceeded with and each one was searched from toes to head. They all took the process coolly.

"The first to go through the hands of the officials was the old man George Edwards, who took his medicine with utmost nonchallance. He is rather a striking looking fellow with grizzled hair and moustache, erect and active and does not appear to bear within ten years of the weight of age which the prison records now credit him with. He claims to be 62, looks like a man of 50, and moves like one of 30. He answered all the questions put to him coolly, but sometimes hesitatingly, evidently considering his answers well. He was asked point blank by one man whether or not he was Bill Miner and his answer was, 'Can't be seeing that I never heard of the man'."

By the following evening the B.C. Police had Pinkerton's description of the noted bandit, Bill Miner. A second examination convinced them that despite Miner's protests, he was indeed the infamous outlaw. Concrete evidence piled up quickly, including a photograph of Miner that arrived from the coast and was identified by mail clerk McQuarrie as that of the man whose mask had slipped during the robbery.

The preliminary hearing opened before Kamloops Mayor Gordon, J.P., on May 17. The prosecution was represented by Attorney General Fulton who was visiting the area, while the defence was conducted by A.D. McIntyre of Kamloops. McIntyre asked for a remand but was refused.

The prosecution's case was straightforward. Engineer Callin positively identified Colquhoun; McQuarrie and Thorburn identified Miner; Constable Fernie and his scouts established the tracking; the police party identified the articles taken from the prisoners as those worn at the robbery.

The subsequent trial on May 28 was a gala event for Kamloops. The court was packed with local curiosity seekers and visitors from as far as Vancouver. Dunn laughed most of the time — a tense, hysterical laugh, while Colquhoun, except for an occasional hacking cough, was quiet. Miner sat stoically through the proceedings. The prisoner's box was too small to hold all three so Shorty Dunn, who had to sit sideways in a chair to ease his wounded leg, sat outside the dock.

With Mr. Justice P.A.E. Irving presiding, the trial opened at 10 a.m. Deputy Attorney-General McLean took his witnesses skillfully through their evidence, while lawyers McIntyre and Murphy sought to discredit the Crown's case. The jury foreman was J. Morrill, a man in his sixties who in many ways bore a resemblance to the chief culprit, Bill Miner.

The evidence with frills and flourishes was identical to that presented at the preliminary hearing. Two days later the case went to the jury. In his summation, Mr. Justice Irving left no doubt that he, at least, was convinced of the guilt of all three. The jury, particularly Morrill, did not all share the judge's view. After four hours of deliberating they stood seven for conviction, five for acquittal. After listening again to several long excerpts from the evidence they retired for further deliberation.

Their indecision was not surprising in view of the joke of the day. "Oh, Bill Miner's not so bad, he only robs the CPR once every two years, but the CPR robs us all every day."

After another seven hours deliberation, the jury announced that it could not agree. It stood eleven to one for conviction. The lone dissenter was foreman Morrill. He had often been heard to delare that a poor man should never be sent to prison.

A new trial was ordered. It opened on June 1 with a new jury under foreman A. McGregor. The evidence, condensed by a weary prosecutor, was presented in two hours, and even this was interrupted on several occasions by hysterical outbursts from Shorty Dunn who broke down and had to be attended by the prison physician.

After deliberating only half an hour, the jury returned a verdict of guilty for all three men. Taking into account Miner's previous record which was attested to by Warden Kelly, brought specifically from San Quentin, and Shorty Dunn's attempt to murder the police party, Mr. Justice Irving sentenced them to life in the grim penitentiary at New Westminster on the coast. Colquhoun, whose only previous known offence was the two-year stint at Walla Walla, was given a stiff twenty-five years. The prisoners accepted their fate without comment.

Although Miner had been extremely successful in many of his previous holdups, this venture had netted only $15 from two registered letters.

On June 3, heavily ironed and under strong escort, the three men waited for the train to take them to the coast. At Kamloops station they were given handfuls of cigars each and appeared in excellent spirits. Noticing Albert Ducks, one of the Crown witnesses, among the crowd, Bill Miner joked: "If I'm ever in the area, I'll look you up."

Of Miner's journey to the jail in New Westminster, *The Kamloops Standard* carried a long report in its June 9 edition. Here are some excerpts:

"Edwards, or Miner, was a subject of considerable interest during the trip. On the way down there were crowds at the depots to catch a glimpse of the prisoners and one woman at Agassiz declared that she recognized Edwards as a man who had once spent the night at her house.

"The men were taken from the train at Sapperton, it being expected that a crowd would congregate if they were removed at New Westminster. There was quite a large assemblage of people at Sapperton and Miner was greeted with shouts of Hello Bill! and How are you Bill? He did not deny his identity. He said I was Mr. Edwards at Kamloops but here everybody, even the dogs seem to know me. Warden Kelly of San Quentin prison, where Miner served a sentence, was also a passenger on the train, and Miner made no effort to conceal his identity to Kelly, as he had done at Kamloops.

"Constable Pearse and Fernie were also interviewed at Vancouver and said the prisoners talked very calmly about their sentences on the way down. Edwards or Miner remarked that he had not very long to live anyhow and he might as well put in his time in the Penitentiary as anywhere else . . . ."

Goodbye, Canada

The penitentiary at New Westminster where Miner was sent for robbing the CPR. Ironically, the jail fronted the CPR's transcontinental main line, a constant reminder to Miner of a robbery which netted $15 cash and a twenty-five-year sentence.
The engine shown in the photo, taken about 1900, brought the first transcontinental train to Vancouver in May 1887.

The prison to which Miner, Dunn and Colquhoun were sent was a constant problem to the Inspector of Penitentiaries in Ottawa. Constructed by the Department of Public Works in 1878, it had no built-in security measures and, worst of all, no outside protective wall. A wooden wall enclosed by a wooden fence was eventually built, but both occasionally fell down,

deliberately pushed or blown by strong winds. Internally, changes were frequent and morale was low. Instead of brutality, however, the low morale produced a listless administration. This listlessness was not helped by the Canadian public's vascillating between punishment and reformation, and at times prison officials had no clear policy to follow. It was often simpler to do nothing. Under these conditions, the B.C. Penitentiary at New Westminster welcomed the notorious Bill Miner — with repercussions which would escalate to the Prime Minister of Canada.

Bill Miner's first months in the penitentiary were ones of close confinement. He was placed in the prison shoe shop, where his first job was to construct a special pair of shoes for his feet. At the end of July 1907, after fourteen months in prison, Miner seemed to have settled down and to have forgotten his promise: "No prison walls can hold me."

A constant visitor to the prisoner's cell was Katherine Bourke, daughter of Deputy Warden Bourke. Attracted by his keen mind and softened by his promise to reform, she persuaded him to dedicate himself to a better life and brought religious literature to read. The Deputy Warden, swayed, no doubt, by his daughter's intercession, relented the maximum

security surrounding the over sixty-year-old robber and had him transferred to the prison brickyard. Miner expressed himself as being supremely happy in his new job and assured the charming Miss Bourke that he was resigned to his fate and no longer cared to escape. Since he was getting old, he said, he would do everything to merit a happier home in the next world.

But on the afternoon of August 8, 1907, Miner suddenly forgot his assurance to Miss Bourke. That afternoon he was working in the prison brickyard, and comparing the friendly attitude of the guards with that of his former keepers in San Quentin. At the time twenty-nine men were at work in the yard. Guard James Doyle supervised two-thirds of the convicts making bricks, while Guard Welsh watched over the remaining prisoners, including Miner, at the drying kiln.

Overlooking the brick kiln and the rest of the yard was a watch tower some 150 feet high from where Guard Alex McNeil commanded a view of the prisoners. From the lookout tower, extending 150 yards in a right angle, was a walk atop the wall which the guard on duty had to patrol every two minutes.

Despite the fact that he was supposed to be infirm and suffering from bad feet, Bill Miner did not grumble as he trundled his wheelbarrow full of bricks from the yard to the drying kiln. It was true that he stopped to rest against the yard fence after each trip, but the sympathetic guards thought nothing of it.

Three inmates who were also wheeling bricks became aware that the prison-wise old con was slowly digging a hole beneath the wooden fence. Soon John Clarke, a young forger serving a three-year sentence, was alternating with Miner, distributing the earth gently around his feet. Albert McCluskey, an old prison hand doing seven years for robbery, began to take a rest at the end of each trip to the kiln. Then Walter John Woods, nervous as a cat, took a turn. Shorty Dunn, working at a brick pile a short distance away, was also aware that Bill was up to something but could not leave his job without attracting attention. Then McNeil provided the opportunity Miner had been waiting for when he disappeared into the wooden room on top of the platform for a furtive cigarette.

Like a rabbit, Miner vanished through the hole under the fence. Woods, Clarke and McCluskey followed. Ahead was the prison's outer wall. Miner, who planned well, led the way to a locked shed containing a ladder. They broke the lock with a pick and placed the ladder against the wall. Then they scrambled over and raced to a fringe of brush a quarter mile away.

About this time, Guard Doyle noticed the discarded wheelbarrows and the hole beneath the fence. He fired his revolver and the prison escape bell clanged a general alarm. It took time, however, to round up the remaining men and return them to their cells, and even more time to secure the rest of the prisoners at work throughout the prison. In fact, it was half an hour before an effective pursuit was organized.

None of the brickyard prisoners admitted they had seen the escape taking place, or that they had knowledge of the escapees' plans. Shorty Dunn was particularly adamant in his denial, while Louis Colquhoun,

$500 Reward

The above reward will be paid for the arrest and detention of WILLIAM (Bill) MINER, alias Edwards, who escaped from the New Westminster Penitentiary, at New Westminster, British Columbia, on the 8th August, 1907, where he was serving a life sentence for train robbery.

DESCRIPTION:

Age 65 years; 138 pounds; 5 feet 8½ inches; dark complexion; brown eyes; grey hair; slight build; face spotted; tattoo base of left thumb, star and ballet girl right forearm; wrist joint-bones large; moles centre of breast, 1 under left breast, 1 on right shoulder, 1 on left shoulder-blade; discoloration left buttock; scars on left shin, right leg, inside, at knee, 2 on neck.

Communicate with

LT.-COL. A. P. SHERWOOD,

Commissioner Dominion Police,
Ottawa, Canada.

The reward poster issued after Miner escaped from New Westminster Penitentiary. His escape caused repercussions that were to involve the Prime Minister of Canada.

confined to the prison hospital where he was to die in 1911 of tuberculosis, seemed pleased but entirely unhelpful. He knew nothing of Bill Miner's plans.

Deputy Warden Bourke averred that no convict in his care had ever remained free for long: "I will have Miner and his three companions behind prison walls within twenty-four hours," he promised.

Bourke felt confident that in view of Miner's bad feet, the old man would drop from exhaustion a short distance from the penitentiary. He had examined Miner's feet only a few days before and had found them in a deplorable condition. Nevertheless, every police center in British Columbia and neighboring Washington was alerted. The Pinkerton Detective Agency in Seattle resignedly opened their files on Bill Miner and, as they had been doing for forty years, circulated his description:

"William A. Miner, alias William Morgan, alias William Anderson; Canadian, occupation shoemaker, weight 138 pounds. Miner's distinguishing marks are on his forearm and were made by a tattooing needle and Indian Ink when he was a youngster; carries a tattoo at the base of thumb of left hand; also a heart pierced with a dagger; a ballet girl is tattooed on his right forearm and also a star; both wrist bones are large; has a mole in center of chest; mole under left breast and another on his right shoulder; another star tattooed on outside of calf of left leg; a discoloration on left buttock; a scar on his left shin; a scar on his right knee. A mole on his left shoulder blade. Two small scars on his neck. His face is pitted and he wears both upper and lower false teeth."

At the penitentiary the trail left by the four escapees was readily discernible for some distance beyond the wall. The prints made by Miner's distinctive shoes were unmistakable. But within a mile of the prison Miner had left his companions for his prints led off in a separate direction.

Of Bill Miner, over sixty, crippled and alone, there was no trace.

The following morning a bloodhound was put on the trail. Given the scent of an old straw hat worn by Miner, the dog started on the escapee's trail but lost it in a field of alfalfa. After two hours of unproductive searching, the chase was abandoned and the bloodhound returned to its kennel.

Prison officials were beginning to fear that if Old Bill Miner, as he was affectionately becoming known in newspaper accounts, evaded immediate capture, his return to prison would be difficult, if not impossible. Although he left $500 in cash, and his fancy watch and chain behind, it was believed he had a large sum of money cached away. For nearly six months a Pinkerton detective had been visiting Shorty Dunn in the penitentiary, supposedly to negotiate the return of $50,000 in U.S. bonds taken during the 1904 train robbery at Mission. With Miner's escape, the detective's visits ceased.

It was also feared that if Miner got clear of the coast, he would find friends and haven in the Nicola Valley where he was remembered as the gentlemanly George Edwards. Certainly public sympathy was on his side in his latest joust with the law. A local newspaper headline read: "Chase of Bill Miner Howling Farce."

That Miner was heading for his former haunts in the Nicola seemed certain when the authorities received a message from farmer George Roche near Abbotsford. Roche was positive that the robber had stopped at his place for dinner on August 12. His visitor's feet were sore, he said, and he was hungry and exhausted. A pursuit was immediately instituted, but there was no trace of the fugitive.

Although Miner himself had successfully disappeared, he left in his wake a controversy that remained for years. Some people felt that he had been deliberately allowed to escape — "handed out" was the expression used to summarize the incident. On February 27, 1909, some eighteen months after Miner's escape, *The Daily Columbian* newspaper at New Westminster noted:

"The conclusion come to at the time was that the convicts escaped through a hole which had been dug under the wall, and which was subsequently detected, but this theory has long since been discarded. Nearly every detective and police officer who inspected the hole said it was impossible for a man to get through it. Many expressed the opinion that the men had gone out through the gate, perhaps with the connivance of friends, and that the hole was dug for a blind."

On March 3 the paper ran a story headed: "EX-WARDEN BOURKE MAKES DEFINITE CHARGES ASSOCIATING COUNSEL OF CONVICT AND C.P.R. DETECTIVE WITH COMPLICITY IN ARRANGING ESCAPE."

The charges arose as a result of persistent rumors that in addition to the gold and other valuables taken during the Mission train robbery there were also Australian bonds which the CPR were anxious to get back. Confirmation that the rumors were valid finally came in the House of Commons on February 11, 1909, when J.D. Taylor, MP and managing director of *The Daily Columbian*, got an admission from Solicitor-General Bureau, despite a previous denial by the Minister of Justice.

As an editorial in the paper noted: "Mr. Aylesworth (the Minister of Justice) disposed of the whole story of irregularities in connection with Miner's escape as entirely without foundation, having arrived at this conclusion from the result reported to him of the investigation carried on by the inspector. He had not heard of any communication with Miner from the outside; in fact, was sure that there had not been any. And the story of the search for securities as an incentive to secure Miner's release he dismissed as shadowy and without foundation. But his excitable colleague the solicitor-general gave the thing away by the admission that detectives had held intercourse with Miner on many occasions and that they were in search of Australian securities taken from the train held up near Mission and possession of which the Canadian Pacific Railway company was most anxious to regain. This admission, extracted from Mr. Bureau after prolonged cross-examination, supplied the key to the whole situation. There was, it appeared, motive for securing the release of Miner; emissaries of the persons having that motive were permitted access to him; and his release did occur. It was the fact, also, that Miner's hair had been allowed to grow, contrary to the practice of keeping the prisoners shorn."

In addition to being permitted to let his hair grow, Miner had been granted other special benefits. These included the right to see his lawyer, Alex D. McIntyre, whenever he desired, to reply "promptly to all letters" instead of being entitled to send one letter a month, to talk to visitors without a prison officer being present, and in the words of a newspaper article, ". . . allowed freedom from the interior of the prison, where criminals of his character are confined, and given the comparative liberty of the brick yard."

He was also offered a pardon, according to Deputy Warden Bourke who was in charge of the prison when Miner escaped. (As a consequence, Bourke was "allowed to retire" and received a retirement allowance of $279.23. McNeil, the guard on the watch tower, was fired.)

Bourke made the statement that Miner was offered a pardon in a letter published in *The Daily Columbian* on March 3, 1909. He said, in part: "On one occasion, the previous summer, 1906, Bill Miner was sent for to go to the Warden's office . . . . He said that he met in the warden's office, the Warden, Lawyer McIntyre, who defended him, C.P.R. Detective Bullock and an old pal of his named Terry, that after a brief conversation the warden went out of the office, that on the warden's going out . . . detective Bullock made an offer of a pardon to Miner if he revealed where the hidden bonds were, and that the C.P.R. would get him the pardon. Miner agreed to this, but wanted a guarantee that the pardon would be forthcoming. The detective could give him no guarantee other than his verbal promise. This Miner would not accept and the interview ended."

Among those who wanted an inquiry into the entire Miner affair was M. Burrell, MP for Yale-Cariboo. In the House of Commons he stated: "The capture of this convict was a credit to the police system of the country and his sentence strengthened the confidence of the public in the administration of justice in Canada and now that he has escaped . . . and in view of the unrest in the public mind about the circumstances of the escape of this notorious criminal, is it not time that we should have an impartial inquiry, not an inquiry at the hands of Inspector Dawson who is hopelessly mixed up in it, but a thorough inquiry by some impartial tribunal."

Even Prime Minister Sir Wilfred Laurier was drawn into the issue. He stated in the House of Commons:

"The question which interests this country . . . is whether there has been any connivance on the part of anybody in the escape of Bill Miner. No more dangerous criminal. I think, was ever in the clutches of Canadian Justice.

"It was a fact for which we took some credit that when one of these American desperadoes came to Canada, thinking to play with impunity in this country the pranks he had been playing on the other side of the line, he was arrested, tried and convicted.

"It was a shock when we heard, and we heard it with a good deal of shame also, that he had been allowed to escape from the penitentiary."

The question of connivance raised by the Prime Minister was never answered. No impartial inquiry was held.

Bill Miner, meanwhile, was probably oblivious of the controversy which still surrounded his escape of nearly two years before. He had disappeared as completely as he had after his first train robbery in Canada. Unfortunately for him, he could not resist the challenge of a railway express car — especially if he had reason to believe it carried gold or greenbacks.

Miner's Last Escape

Below: Convicts in Georgia in 1911, their legs shackled in chains tied to a belt at the waist. For his role in Georgia's first train holdup, Miner was sentenced to work on a similar "ball and chain" gang, although he was then sixty-eight.

After Miner's escape from New Westminster penitentiary, the B.C. Provincial Police and Pinkertons kept their files on him open, although the last entry in either file concerned the visit to Roche's farm. There was a brief flurry of interest in June 1909 when the Imperial Limited was held up seven miles east of Ducks by the same method that Bill had used in 1906. The holdup proved to be the work of brothers Bill and David Haney. Dave was accosted near Ashcroft, B.C., by Provincial Police Constable Decker. In the ensuing gun battle, both Haney and Decker were killed. Bill Haney fled and was reportedly never captured.

A close watch was kept on Jack Budd's Ranch at Princeton, but Miner never appeared. As had been feared, he vanished.

In later years Bill supplied a few meagre details of his whereabouts during the two years following his escape. He claimed to have fled to the United States and worked in a mine. After a short period of hiding, he emerged to take part in an express train holdup in Oregon which financed a trip to Europe. After getting into difficulty with bank officials on the Continent, he claimed to have returned to the States and taken a job in

Pennsylvania. During this period, he called himself George Anderson and posed as a southern gentleman in search of health.

Those who knew Miner intimately disbelieved every word he said about his activities following his successful prison break. Incredible as his true career was, Miner was forever embellishing it with fictitious exploits. At one time he claimed to have been a member of the Jesse James' gang — but records prove that he was in San Quentin at the time. Though he served almost twenty years in San Quentin on his third sentence, he claimed to have served only ten and to have been secretly released by prison officials to commit a special robbery.

It is known that Miner, alias George Anderson, got himself a job looking after electrical equipment in a small Pennsylvania sawmill. He was a good worker and was well thought of. But his eye was forever roving and his brain was forever churning. Miner was pacing himself now, reserving the strength remaining in a slender, wiry body ravaged by long periods of confinement and hardship. Although now over sixty-six, his slow movements belied the energy beneath a calm exterior. His steely blue eyes still calculated the world from under shaggy gray brows and his soft white mustache continued to give the impression of a kindly old man. But he hadn't changed. Ever on the lookout for an accomplice, he made himself acquainted with Charles Hunter, a young sawmill hand. That Miner's leadership qualities also hadn't deteriorated was obvious when in the spring of 1910 the two men left their sawmill jobs and headed south.

In Virginia, Miner's uncanny sense of people led him to George Handsford, another sawmill hand. The trio continued southward and by the end of 1910 all were employed at a sawmill in Lula, Georgia. The camp was located conveniently near the main line of the Southern Express.

On the night of February 22, 1911, Bill Miner led his two men towards the railway tracks. Well armed and masked, they flagged the New Orleans to New York Southern Express at White Sulphur Springs, near Gainesville in Georgia, and pushed pistols into the faces of the crew. A small safe in the baggage car yielded $1,000 when blown open with dynamite but a large one containing $65,000 in gold resisted three separate explosions. Bill had failed to master the modern techniques of safe blowing, although he did have the distinction of committing the first train robbery in the state of Georgia.

Miner divided the plunder and the three men separated. Hunter and Hansford travelled north together but Old Man Miner, still the loner, turned south.

With the meagre descriptions supplied by the trainmen, posses scoured the timbered countryside. Two days after the holdup, a posse came upon a deserted looking cabin near Gainsville occupied by an old man who vaguely resembled the description of the leader of the gang. He was obviously in poor health and looked a most unlikely suspect. The posse, however, tired and annoyed after their long, fruitless chase decided to take him in as proof of their diligence. George Anderson, as the old man called himself, laughed at the idea of being a suspected train robber and willingly accompanied the posse. At Gainesville he was turned over to the local police. They reluctantly locked him up and continued trying to locate the real bandits.

Two days later a Pinkerton detective assigned to the case happened to notice the old man lounging comfortably in the country prison. There was something familiar about his features. The detective played a hunch and checked his files. Suddenly he realized who the old man was. It took only a moment to uncover the dancing girl tattooed on Miner's right arm.

Despite this positive identification, and the certainty of deportation to Canada to serve the balance of his life sentence, Bill Miner stoutly avowed innocence in the Georgia train robbery. Even when his two companions were arrested and confessed, naming him as the leader, he maintained his smiling, benevolent silence.

On March 11, 1911, in the Gainesville courtroom, Hunter and Hansford pleaded guilty. In a last minute effort to secure a reduced sentence by confessing, Miner told the story of planning the robbery in Pennsylvania and carrying it out. The sixty-eight-year old man was nevertheless sentenced to twenty years, his companions to fifteen each.

Miner was held at Gainsville for a week while officials debated his fate. Application had been made by the Canadian authorities to have him returned to New Westminster to serve his life term. Bill himself favored this plan. He told newspaper reporters that he feared rough treatment from the Georgia prison system and would prefer to be returned to Canada where he had been treated so kindly. W.M. Pinkerton, who had once labelled the old rascal the master criminal of the American West, declared that Miner was too sly to remain confined for long in a county jail or a prison camp. He recommended his return to the maximum security prison in Canada.

Confident of their own prison system, Georgia officials decided to hold him. His age and obvious ill health convinced them that he was not dangerous. Unfortunately, they also greatly underestimated the amazing stamina of the nearly seventy-year-old Miner. He was first sent to the Newton County chain gang and later transferred to the Milledgeville State Prison Farm.

Bill Miner began his long prison term in the Georgia convict camp with the quiet conviction that unless he took desperate measures he would assuredly die in prison. Like many habitual criminals, he had a fear — almost a mania — of dying behind bars. Conscious of his failing strength, he looked around for a strong companion.

The prison warders, basically kind men beneath harsh exteriors, gradually let their hearts dictate their treatment of the celebrated train robber. They relaxed their vigilance, all the opportunity Miner needed.

Papers throughout North America related what happened. The October 21, 1911, issue of *The Denver Republican* in Colorado carried a headline "HIGHWAYMAN OF MANY ALIASES AT LIBERTY," and went on to note:

"A man with a brand new alias is likely to appear at one of Denver's fashionable hotels within the next few days. He will be a man of about 65 years, 5 feet 9½ inches in height, with gray hair, gray mustache, brown eyes, and a long thin nose, weighing about 146 pounds, wearing clothes of noisy design and more than fashionable cut. He will probably wear diamonds of unusual size. And, if he can arrange it, he will be seen frequently in the immediate vicinity of other lovers of fashion.

"If he is not fortunate he will be handcuffed by the first hotel detective who sees him, or by one of the Pinkerton detectives. If he is captured, he will be sent back to Milledgeville, Georgia, to serve out a 20-year sentence for robbing a Southern Railway train . . . ."

On October 18, 1911, scarcely seven months after the prison gates closed behind him, Miner and a fellow prisoner, Tom Moore, had overpowered a guard and fled. Despite his crippled feet and failing strength, Miner led his young companion through almost uninhabited country towards St. Clair, Moore's home community. It was Moore who faded first beneath the hardship by succumbing to swamp fever. With fanatical determination the old man urged him on.

Staggering, swearing, praying, they made their way through the desolate country, at times holding their breaths as posses with bloodhounds passed near them. Seventeen days later, skeletons of their former selves, they holed up in a boxcar on the outskirts of St. Clair, almost within sight of Moore's home. They were seen and a posse which had been following them surrounded the freight car. Moore recklessly opened fire with a revolver he had stolen. The police returned fire, riddling the boxcar. Miner kept firing until Moore dropped dead from a police bullet. Then he threw his revolver out and surrendered.

Milledgeville prison officials took no chances once Miner was in their hands again. They locked a ball and chain on the celebrated escapee, confirming that despite his poor health and advanced age, they considered Miner their most dangerous charge.

It seemed impossible that Old Bill — one foot in the grave, the other secured by ball and chain — could escape again. But as had happened many times previously, prison officials underestimated Miner's determination. Incredibly, on the night of June 29, 1912, during a thunderstorm he managed to cut his shackles, saw the bars from his prison window and disappear into the rain with two cell mates.

Once again the county sheriffs organized pursuit parties. When the rain cleared, bloodhounds picked up the scent of the three convicts leading to the Oconee swamp but lost it when it became evident that Miner and his companions had stolen a boat and were running down river. Somewhere along the way, the boat overturned and one of the men drowned.

How the old man kept going in a swamp infested with poisonous snakes and devoid of food and shelter was nothing short of miraculous. But once again Fate spread a protective mantle over the old man. Having lost one companion through drowning, he lost the other when he slowed the flight and his fellow escapee went on ahead. Half starved, half mad from the nightmare of fighting the swamp, crippled feet in pitiable condition, Bill Miner staggered from the swamps at McIntyre into the arms of the posse.

This time, his powers of recuperation failed. In the prison hospital, he lingered, fighting desperately to regain the strength for one last battle for freedom. But the vitality was gone. On the evening of September 2, 1913, Bill Miner died. The local paper called it his ". . . third escape from the Georgia penitentiary, this time in company with the angel of death."

But even as the old bandit lay dead he wasn't deserted by the good fortune that had protected him from being lynched like his companion robber in Colorado, or shot to death with his fellow escapee in Georgia.

Since prison officials could find no relatives, Miner's body would have gone to the medical school except for Joseph Alfred Moore who owned a funeral home in Milledgeville.

"Mr. Joe" as Moore was called, taught Sunday school at Milledgeville Prison. Like the Deputy Warden's daughter at New Westminster seven years before he had been impressed with Miner, considering him a gentleman compared with the general crowd of convicts. "Mr. Joe bought a casket for Bill Miner and donated his time," a long-time employee of the funeral home recalled in 1982.

He also provided a burial plot, while other citizens contributed to buy clothes and Reverend H.L.J. Williams, pastor of the Episcopal Church, read the funeral service. Then pallbearers and even City Officials followed "Mr. Joe's" hearse down Liberty Street to Milledgeville's cemetery on Memory Hill. While it was an impressive funeral for the penniless "Hands-up" bandit, it was a confinement which even for him there was no escape.

For some reason the location of Miner's plot was omitted from cemetery records. Nearly half a century passed and it seemed that he would join thousands of other criminals whose graves are unknown. Then Dr. James C. Bonner, a respected Georgia historian, paid for a tombstone. After some fifty years the quiet-spoken bandit was still able to find a friend, although the stone cutter erred in the year of Miner's death. He died in 1913.

Official RNWMP Report of Miner's Capture

In charge of the RNWMP contingent in the 1906 search for Bill Miner and his two companions was Sergeant J.J. Wilson. On May 19 he gave the following report to Superintendent R.B. Deane, Commander of "E" Division in Calgary:

According to instructions I left Calgary on the afternoon of May 11 with Sergeant Thomas, Corporals Stewart, Peters and Constable Tabuteau, picking up Constable Browning and Sergeant Shoebotham at Morley and Banff. We arrived at Kamloops about 3 p.m., of the 12th, and having our own saddles and bridles, we were supplied with local horses, two of which were old and broken up, the rest were almost unbroken bronchos and only the coolness and careful handling by the men prevented some serious accidents.

We left Kamloops at 6 p.m., patrolling south, arriving at a ranch about twenty miles out at 12.30. Our horses were played out, the night dark and wet. It was impossible to go further so we camped for the night with a rancher named Blackburn.

At daylight of the 13th, I tried to get a fresh horse for Sergeant

The Royal North West Mounted Policemen who captured the Miner gang after they had been found by Provincial Constable W. Fernie. Sitting, left to right: Constable J. Tabuteau, Staff Sergeant J.J. Wilson, and Corporal C.R. Peters. Standing, left to right: Sergeant Thomas, guide Jim Benyon, Sergeant Shoebotham, Corporal Stewart and Constable Browning. The officers all wore civilian clothes during the search.

Shoebotham, whose horse was very much played out the night before, but was unable to do so. We therefore had to travel slowly at first. We travelled across country towards Douglas lake, making inquiries at every ranch and every person we saw. We fed the horses every chance we got and this seemed to freshen the horse ridden by Sergeant Shoebotham and we began to make better time. We arrived at Douglas lake about 5 p.m. on Sunday the 13th, and after making inquiries there, I concluded that the only likely place for the robbers to be was between Chapperon lake, Salmon lake and Campbell meadows (where the men were last seen).

I obtained a pack outfit from Mr. Greaves, manager of the Douglas lake ranch. Sent telephone message to the Commissioner to this effect but subsequently learned message was not received by him.

At daylight on morning of 14th, we patrolled to Chapperon lake, where I intended to start for Campbell meadows. Just after having lunch, Provincial Constable Fernie rode up and said he had seen three men on foot with packs on their backs, whose description agreed with that of the train robbers. He could not describe where he had seen them but could take us there. My party immediately galloped off, making the 7 miles in about 20 minutes. Fernie showed us where he had seen the men but we could find no tracks, and he could not tell which way they were going when he saw them last.

I obtained the assistance of an Indian tracker. Constable Browning saw some tracks on the trail going towards Quilchena, but the Indian concluded they were Chinaman's tracks.

I then sent Sergeant Thomas up a mountain to see if he could observe anything from there. Constable Tabuteau with the guide Jim Benyon and the Indian I sent back to where the robbers came from to try and get track of them. Provincial Constable Fernie in the meantime had gone on to

Douglas lake. The rest of my party scattered out to patrol towards Quilchena.

After going about a mile and a half, Corporal Stewart, who was to the left of the patrol and a little ahead, waved his hat. Sergeant Shoebotham and myself with Corporal Peters and Constable Browning, immediately galloped towards Corporal Stewart, where he had seen smoke in the brush.

We all dismounted, leaving the horses standing, went in to the brush and found three men eating dinner. I asked them where they came from. The eldest man, who afterwards gave the name of Edwards, said 'Across the river.'

I asked them where they were before that. Edwards said 'From over there' (pointing towards Campbell meadows). I asked how long since they had left there. Edwards said 'Two days.' I then asked them what they were doing. The one who afterwards gave the name of Dunn, answered, 'Prospecting a little.' I then said, 'You answer the description given of the train robbers and we arrest you for that crime.'

Edwards said, 'We do not look much like train robbers.' Just then Dunn rolled over and said, 'Look out boys, it is all up,' and commenced to fire his revolver.

I immediately covered Edwards. Corporal Peters was standing close to Colquhoun, who was reaching for his revolver, and he covered him and ordered him to put up his hands, at the same time snatching away Colquhoun's revolver.

Sergeant Shoebotham, Corporal Stewart and Constable Browning ran after Dunn, firing as they went, he returned the fire as he ran. After some twenty shots had been exchanged Dunn fell into a ditch and threw up his hands, saying, 'I am shot.' The men ceased firing and took two revolvers from Dunn. On taking him out of the ditch it was found he had been shot in the calf of the leg, the bullet going right through.

I told him he had done a foolish thing as he might have got shot in the head instead of the leg. He said, 'I wish to _____ you had put it through my head, but you couldn't blame me, could you?'

I then had Dunn's leg bandaged up and sent a messenger to get a rig to convey the prisoners to jail. I also sent the guide Benyon to Quilchena to get the Commissioner on the telephone and tell him all the particulars. This message I subsequently learned was taken by Supt. Hussey of the provincial police in Commissioner Perry's name. I also sent word to Benyon to send a doctor out to meet us, as I did not know how much of Dunn's drawers might be left in the wound.

The prisoners were then searched, and the hands of Edwards and Colquhoun bound. Three automatic revolvers, one 44 Colt's (six chamber), one Ivor Johnson 38, one Smith & Wesson 38, and one Winchester carbine 44 were found in their effects.

The goggles worn by Edwards were found in his coat pocket. A small bottle of catarrh cure, which was supposed to have been from the mail car was found among their effects. Very little money was found on them. Edwards had one ten dollar gold piece, one five dollar bill, one ten dollar bill and two fifty cent pieces. The other two prisoners only had some small silver on them.

56

A team having arrived, the prisoners were conveyed to Douglas Lake ranch, where I had Dunn's leg washed, camphor ice put on and bandaged up. We then fed the horses and obtained lunch from Mr. Greaves, also a team and light democrat. Left about 5 p.m., for Quilchena, meeting Dr. Tuthill about four miles out of Quilchena. After a short consultation with the doctor and prisoner Dunn, we concluded to go on to Quilchena before doing anything to the leg. After arriving at Quilchena the doctor dressed the wound, first probing and finding no bones broken, the bullet passing through the fleshy part of the right leg. A message by this time had come to me supposedly from Commissioner Perry to hold the men till he came out to Quilchena, where he would be at daylight. The message was afterwards changed. It was Superintendent Hussey who was coming out. I then tried to get the Commissioner on the telephone but was unable to do so.

I then detailed a night guard of two men over the prisoners, the rest of the men sleeping in the same building. At daylight on the 15th, I made ready to start to Kamloops, a distance of fifty miles. At Rockford, fifteen miles away from Quilchena, I met Superintendent Hussey, who wanted to take the prisoners away from us. He did not succeed, however, and we arrived at Kamloops about 5 p.m. in a pouring rain, and delivered the prisoners and their effects over to the provincial jail.

On the 16th instant, the prisoners were remanded till 10 a.m., of the 17th. On the 17th, Sergeants Wilson and Shoebotham, Corporals Stewart and Peters and Constable Browning gave evidence, and at 6 a.m., of the 18th, Sergeant Wilson and party left for Calgary arriving here at 1.30 p.m. In conclusion I wish respectfully to draw your attention to the good work done by every member of my party, work done for the most part in a pouring rain and darkness. The distance covered was about 185 miles in three days and nights. I would especially draw your attention to the work of Sergeant Shoebotham, Corporals Stewart and Peters and Constable Browning. Their coolness and courage under fire from an automatic revolver I think, could not be surpassed.

I would also draw your attention to the kind assistance received by us from Mr. J.B. Greaves, manager of the Douglas Lake ranch who told us to go to any of his camps, of which there are several, and get anything we wanted. It is such assistance that makes arduous police duty lighter.

The man Dunn told me before leaving to tell all members of the North-west Mounted Police, that he had no grievance against any of them, they had done their duty well and he was thankful for the kind attention which he received after being wounded, and he said, you may think it funny coming from me, but I certainly admire the way you boys do your work.

On the train coming home I met a man named C.J. Hawes, who recognized Colquhoun from a photograph we had, and said he went to college with him. Hawes thought he might be able to do something with Colquhoun as to getting the truth out of him, so I gave him a note to Mr. Clauss, who is acting with the attorney general.

Edwards has been positively identified by Mail Clerk McQuarrie as one of the men who held him up. He has also been recognized as Bill Miner, who is supposed to have had a hand in the Mission Junction hold-up. He is also wanted badly in several places in the United States.

Constable Fernie's Account of Tracking the Miner Gang

The posse of B.C. Provincial Police, special constables and Indian trackers who played a major role in capturing Miner. From left to right: Tracker Alec Ignace, Constable William Fernie, Constable E. Pearse, tracker Michel Lakama, Ernie Carter, Constable Young holding dog, E. La Roux, Douglas Lake Ranch manager Joe Greaves, Louis Campbell and tracker Philip Thomas.

The May 19, 1906, issue of The Kamloops Standard *carried the following account of the part played by Constable Fernie, one of the key men in the search:*

Provincial Constable W. L. Fernie, who has all along shown untiring energy in tracking the robbers, and who is certainly entitled to the lion's share of the reward is too well known in Kamloops to make any lengthy description necessary. Before the outbreak of the Boer War he was a rancher on the North Thompson. When the first contingent of the Strathcona Horse was raised he joined that body and accompanied it to South Africa and was present all through the campaign.

On his return to British Columbia he received the appointment of Provincial constable, and has since been stationed here.

Constable Fernie tells his own story of the events which led up to the capture of the desperadoes on Thursday afternoon last.

"When the news of the holdup arrived at Kamloops," he said, "Constable Pearse and others went back on an engine to the scene of the robbery while I and an Indian followed the north bank of the river, in case

the robbers should have crossed by boat. Not seeing any trace of them on that bank I came over, and at daylight stumbled upon one of their camps. I particularly noticed the marks their boots made on the dry soil. There were two of the men with miner's boots — hobnailed — while the third had lighter soled. I followed these tracks back some distance and plainly saw where the men had come down the hill. With me then was an Indian, and we came upon the same three pair of footprints facing the other way. These new tracks were much fresher, and I knew then that we were on the right scent. Night came and again at daylight we started out. I had not heard from any of the other posses and did not know how the chase was progressing in other directions.

"After losing the trail many times and retracing our steps, sometimes going back as far as eight or ten miles to pick up the scent, we came upon Dalton's old cabin which is now disused and which had been boarded up. The Indians could only just get a glimmer of the tracks now and again, and as we were not at all sure whether our quarry was in the deserted cabin we took great precautions. I worked toward the back of the shanty to see if there was any exit or window, and was just coming round to the front when I caught sight of one of the Indians gesticulating and signalling to me to be cautious. I had crept up to the door of the hut and had found that a new padlock which had fastened the door was lying on the ground broken. Sneaking up to the door quietly and stationing an Indian on either side I threw open the door and finally expected that the men we were chasing would rush out. But no one was there. Inside all was confusion and the robbers had evidently turned everything upside down in a vain attempt to get a change of clothing.

"We could not find any trace of the trio from within a short distance of the hut.

"The tracks led to a road and there completely vanished. Up and down this road we searched, probably going backward and forward a dozen times. Then suddenly the Indian gave an ejaculation of triumph. Nearly buried in the dust and only visible after the most minute examination, were peculiar dents which could not have been made by an animal and yet occurred at regular intervals along the road. The Indian with smiles upon his face started to walk across the road on his heels, and exultingly pointed out that this was how we had been baffled. The robbers whenever they had come to a road had taken this method of covering their tracks.

"Our horses were worn out, and exhausted, but only camping at nightfall we doggedly stuck to the trail. I sent word to Pearse of how we had traced these tracks and pushed on. We came upon the camp where the robbers had left their saddles. There were the remains of the fire, and littered about were tin pans and other utensils for cooking.

"We withdrew and watched the camp on the chance that our quarry might return. In the bush, which was very thick around here, we came upon two horses that had been hobbled. These two horses were commandeered by the posse and were ridden right through to the conclusion of the chase.

"The bloodhounds which had been promised us had not arrived and I sent word to hurry them so that we could take up the trail fresh from this camp. After much searching I again found the tracks and traced them up a steep mountain. Here I found a place that had evidently been used as a lookout by one of the gang. Stuck in a crevice of the rock were two candles half burned. On the south, which had been much disturbed, were the ever-recurring tracks of the hob-nailed miners' boots. These ended abruptly and it was evident that this place had only been used by one of the trio, on guard.

"Saturday came and with it drenching rain which made it doubly difficult to trace the tracks. However, we managed to follow them, though they were blurred and indistinct for nearly ten miles in a southerly direction. We then met a man who said he knew the trails about that part, and after wandering in a winding fashion along these and not finding any trace of the robbers we came to the conclusion that they must be old trappers' trails. Back we went and picked up the old scent again. This time we managed with difficulty to trace it and it seemed to be making for a high peak. We decided to cut across country to the knoll which we could see in the distance. There was thick brush in the way and often we had to hew our track with an axe. When we were nearly at our destination we unfortunately struck a deep swamp and in spite of efforts of the Indians to find a way across or around, we had to admit defeat, retrace our steps and follow the trail around.

"That night, tired and wet, we camped at the peak. Our horses were nearly done up and we wondered if in the morning they would be fit to continue. During the night it snowed and when we shook ourselves out of our blankets in the morning there was an inch of snow over us. The new trail ran down to Stevens ranch and we arrived there about one o'clock that morning. Stevens said that he had seen the men and knew of a trail they had blazed in the neighborhood so Constable Pearse stayed to investigate . . . .

"I rode on and made Fish Lake that night. At Tom Jones' house they told how they had been sitting quietly around the fire when a Chinaman suddenly exclaimed that a man was looking through the door. When they rushed out, however, no trace of the intruder could be found, and an examination of the stables showed nothing missing. I have not the slightest doubt, however, that this was one of the robbers, who made tracks when the Chinaman shouted.

"I made Graves' ranch and found that the Mounted Police had been there and had received instructions to join Pearse at Chapperon Lake. When about two miles from Douglas Lake I saw three men coming along packing something white. At first I thought they were Siwashes but when I got closer I saw that they were the men that were wanted.

"It was too late to turn back, for they had seen me almost at the same instant, so I trudged on towards them. They hailed me, Edwards asking: 'Hello! Which is the way to Quilchena?'

"I pointed out the direction to him and queried them. 'Am I on the right road for Chapperon?' They replied to my question and in an affable way I asked where they came from.

" 'Oh, we're prospectors,' said the old man, who seemed to be the most nonchalant and the spokesman of the party. 'We've been to Grande Prairie.'

"After passing the time of day with them I started to walk on, and noticed a movement of the younger man. He had had one hand in his pocket during the whole of the conversation, and through his coat I could see the outline of an automatic pistol. Sticking out of the other man's pocket I could see another revolver. Pretending not to notice these glaring evidences of their identity, I trudged on and never looked back until nearly over a hill. They were continuing in the same direction as when I first saw them.

"Quickly making a detour, I arrived back at Graves', got a fresh horse and a rifle and galloped madly to Chapperon. There I found the Mounted Police unsaddled for the night. Hastily telling them the situation — they were saddled up and well under way in less than three minutes — I guided them back to the place where I had met the robbers. There we spread out and searched the brush which is very thick.

"We were unable to find the men and I decided that it would be well to have the blood hounds sent to this point, so I rode off to Douglas Lake for a messenger. I heard the firing shortly after and when I came back found the bandits were under arrest."

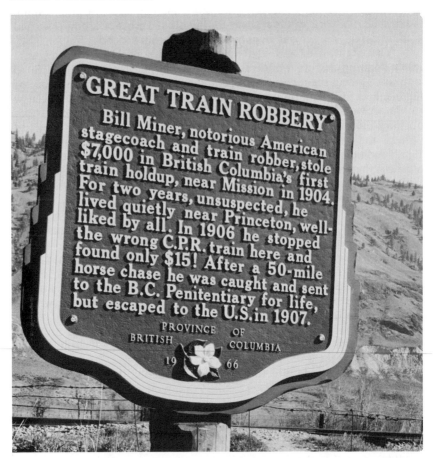

A Stop-of-Interest plaque on the Trans-Canada Highway near Monte Creek east of Kamloops today commemorates Miner's disastrous second train holdup in B.C.

A selection of other *HERITAGE HOUSE* titles:

The PIONEER DAYS IN BRITISH COLUMBIA Series
Every article is true, many written or narrated by those who, 100 or more years ago, lived the experiences they relate. Each volume contains 160 pages in large format magazine size (8½ x 11"), four-color covers, some 60,000 words of text and over 200 historical photos, many published for the first time.

A continuing Canadian best seller in four volumes which have sold over 75,000 copies. Each volume, $11.95

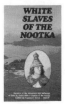

WHITE SLAVES OF THE NOOTKA
On March 22, 1803, while anchored in Nootka Sound on the West Coast of Vancouver Island, the *Boston* was attacked by "friendly" Nootka Indians. Twenty-five of her 27 crew were massacred, their heads "arranged in a line" for survivor John Jewitt to identify. Jewitt and another survivor became 2 of 50 slaves owned by Chief Maquina, never knowing what would come first — rescue or death.

The account of their ordeal, published in 1815, remains remarkably popular. New Western Canadian edition, well illustrated. 128 pages. $9.95

THE DEATH OF ALBERT JOHNSON: Mad Trapper of Rat River
Albert Johnson in 1932 triggered the greatest manhunt in Canada's Arctic history. In blizzards and numbing cold he was involved in four shoot-outs, killing one policeman and gravely wounding two other men before being shot to death.

This revised, enlarged edition includes photos taken by "Wop" May, the legendary bush pilot whose flying skill saved two lives during the manhunt. Another Canadian best seller. $7.95

OUTLAWS AND LAWMEN OF WESTERN CANADA
These true police cases prove that our history was anything but dull. Chapters in 160-page Volume Three, for instance, include Saskatchewan's Midnight Massacre, The Yukon's Christmas Day Assassins, When Guns Blazed at Banff, and Boone Helm — The Murdering Cannibal.

Each of the three volumes in this Canadian best seller series is well illustrated with maps and photos and four-color photos on the covers. Volume One, $8.95; Volume Two, $8.95; Volume Three, $9.95

B.C. PROVINCIAL POLICE STORIES: Mystery and Murder
from the Files of Western Canada's First Lawmen
The B.C. Police, born in 1858, were the first lawmen in Western Canada. During their 90 years of service they established a reputation as one of the most progressive police forces in North America. All cases in this best selling title are reconstructed from archives and police files by ex-Deputy Commissioner Cecil Clark who served on the force for 35 years.

Volume One: 16 chapters, many photos, 128 pages. $8.95
Volume Two: 22 chapters, many photos, 144 pages. $9.95

B.C. BACKROADS
This best selling series contains complete information from Vancouver through the Fraser Canyon to Cache Creek, east to Kamloops country and north to the Cariboo. Also from Vancouver to Bridge River-Lillooet via Whistler. Each book contains mile-by-mile route mileage, history, fishing holes, wildlife, maps and photos.

Volume One — Garibaldi to Bridge River Country-Lillooet. $9.95
Volume Three — Junction Country: Boston Bar to Clinton. $9.95
Thompson-Cariboo: Highways, byways, backroads. $5.95

An Explorer's Guide: MARINE PARKS OF B.C.

To tens of thousands of boaters, B.C.'s Marine Parks are as welcome an convenient as their popular highway equivalents. This guide include anchorages and onshore facilities, trails, picnic areas, campsites, histo and other information. In addition, it is profusely illustrated with col and black and white photos, maps and charts.

Informative reading for boat owners from runabouts to cabin cruiser
200 pages. **$12.9**

GO FISHING WITH THESE BEST SELLING TITLES

HOW TO CATCH SALMON — BASIC FUNDAMENTALS

The most popular salmon book ever written. Information on trolling, riggin tackle, most productive lures, proper depths, salmon habits, how to pla and net your fish, downriggers, where to find fish.
Sales over 120,000. 176 pages. $5.95

HOW TO CATCH SALMON — ADVANCED TECHNIQUES

The most comprehensive advanced salmon fishing book available. Ove 200 pages crammed full of how-to tips and easy-to-follow diagrams. Cove all popular salmon fishing methods: mooching, trolling with bait, spoon and plugs, catching giant chinook, and much more.
A continuing best seller. 192 pages. $11.95

HOW TO CATCH CRABS: How popular is this book? This is the 11 printing, with sales over 90,000. $4.95

HOW TO CATCH BOTTOMFISH: Revised and expanded. $4.95

HOW TO CATCH SHELLFISH: Updated 4th printing. 144 pages. $3.95

HOW TO CATCH TROUT by Lee Straight, one of Canada's to outdoorsmen. 144 pages. $5.95

HOW TO COOK YOUR CATCH: Cooking seafood on the boat, in a campe or at the cabin. 8th printing. 192 pages. $4.95

FLY FISH THE TROUT LAKES

with Jack Shaw
Professional outdoor writers describe the author as a man "who can com away regularly with a string when everyone else has been skunked." I this book, he shares over 40 years of studying, raising and photographin all forms of lake insects and the behaviour of fish to them.
Written in an easy-to-follow style. 96 pages. $7.95

A CUTTHROAT COLLECTION: B.C. experts pool their knowledge an experience to unravel the mysteries and methods of catching this elusiv fish. $5.95

SALMON FISHING BRITISH COLUMBIA: Volumes One and Two

Since B.C. has some 7,000 miles of coastline, a problem to its 400,00 salmon anglers is where to fish. These books offer a solution. Volum One includes over 100 popular fishing holes around Vancouver Island Volume Two covers the Mainland Coast from Vancouver to Jervis Inlet Both include maps, gear to use, best times, lures and a tackle box ful of other information.
Volume One — Vancouver Island. $9.95
Volume Two — Mainland Coast: Vancouver to Jervis Inlet. $11.95

Heritage House books are sold throughout Western Canada. If not availabl at your bookstore you may order direct from Heritage House, Box 1228 Station A, Surrey, B.C. V3S 2B3. Payment can be by cheque or money orde but add 7 per cent for the much hated GST. Books are shipped postpaid.